ANGER

NANCY SHIFFRIN

MAJOR BOOKS • CHATSWORTH, CALIFORNIA

Contents

Chapter One

The Healthy Expression of Anger

There is a crucial relationship between the ability to feel anger and a person's entire sense of emotional and even physical well-being. When you are aware of feeling displeasure or annoyance, you may notice a bodily warmth, as blood vessels dilate and nerve endings are stimulated. You may notice flushing and a rapid heartbeat.

You may have a desire to hit, to shout, to use strong language. You certainly want others to know how you feel. Ideally, at this point, some communication with the person who has offended you will take place.

Recognizing Your Feelings

You know that your experience of anger is healthy when you are willing to recognize it; many people will do anything rather than acknowledge their own displeasure.

Before you can even begin to consider a healthy and appropriate expression of your feelings, you must recognize your own anger signs. You may often express disappointment, frustration, let-down, anxiety, and depression, unaware that the basis may be repressed anger.

When your emotions are *acceptable* to you, you have taken the first step in the journey toward a healthy expression of them. Guilt and fear are tremendous blocks.

In the beginning stages of getting in touch with your feelings, it may not be possible for you to attack the problem directly. If you are tense, depressed, or even sad, it may be valuable to ask yourself what you may be angry about. Just keep an open mind about the possibility that what is *really* bothering you and remains unresolved is anger hiding behind another emotion.

Reason

"How can I be angry with you, you've given me no reason," a client said to me, when I suggested to her that I might be the source of her irritation that day. By definition, anger is not reasonable. You will block your feeling of it if the source must be reasonable. What you will want to know, later on, after you've acknowledged your feeling, is whether or not its *expression* is appropriate at a given time. Keep in mind that there is a big difference between feeling and expressing.

What has really upset you? Is it your little girl's squeaky voice? Or did your boss give you a hard time at work, and your little girl's voice is only the last straw? When you are consistently identifying and expressing displeasure at its true source, you are on the way to a healthy emotional experience.

A number of things make it difficult for you to locate the source of your anger.

The person who has really enraged you may be stronger and more powerful than you are. You may imagine that you have too much to lose by confronting that person. Your child is more vulnerable.

You may not want to admit that you made a mistake. If you gave your son the wrong answer on his homework, you may be angry with yourself when he points it out the next day. It may be easier to take it out on him.

You may feel guilty. Perhaps you are resentful of your mother. You have been taught that motherhood is sacred, that you may not be angry with your mother. The sight of *any* older woman may annoy you.

Perhaps someone else's good intentions intimidate you. "But my mother didn't know she was educating me to be passive and incompetent," a female client said to me, "how can I possibly resent her." What you feel is what you feel; its reasonableness and justifiablity are separate issues. When you can separate the two, you are on your way to emotional health.

Once you have recognized your feeling, and located the source of it, you are ready to look at the mechanics of how someone or something displeases you.

If someone hits you, even by accident, you are annoyed because you are in pain. Even if the person apologized, your feeling might remain for awhile. Pain makes you angry.

If you are a woman and a strange man approaches you with an invitation to have sex, you are irritated because someone is trying to take advantage of you. Being taken advantage of makes you angry.

These are the more obvious mechanics.

Anger, because it is so unacceptable to many people, can hide itself in many subtle ways. Take the case of Jane Snow. Jane is a middle-aged woman who suffers from hypochondria. Her daughter, Cheryl, had been devoting her whole life to tending to Jane's imaginary illnesses. On the surface, mother and daughter seemed to love each other.

Cheryl had an opportunity to get married. Her fiance, however, did not want to spend his life tending Jane. He suggested counseling for all of them.

As it turned out, Jane resented her own mother, long dead. She was punishing Cheryl instead, creating a situation in which Cheryl felt obligated to function as the devoted mother Jane never had.

The relationship between Jane and Cheryl, was, of course, far from a genuinely loving one. Once Jane was able to acknowledge her long-repressed feelings toward her own mother, she was able to accept Cheryl's anger toward her. Together, mother and daughter were able to give up the destructive game they were playing with each other. The relationship became a valuable, healthy one, and Cheryl's marriage had a chance of working.

Sometimes, rage may be a result of personalizing slights or discourtesies that weren't directed at you as an individual. You become furious and say to yourself, "Why do things like this always happen to me?" You will know that your emotions are healthy when you are angry with the rudeness, and say so, at the same time realizing that the incident was not personal, that the offending person would be rude to anyone.

Getting into Reality

Once you have accepted your anger, recognized it, located its source, and understood the mechanics of it, you can begin the process of dealing with it realistically.

When the cause is realistic—for example, someone pushes ahead of you in line—a simple, direct confrontation may be the answer. You may ask the person to go to the rear of the line. You are not dealing with reality when you swallow your feelings in such situations.

Appropriateness

When the amount of feeling coming out of you seems proportionate to the issue at hand, you are expressing yourself appropriately. When the amount of feeling is excessive, you are probably tapping into your savings account of repressed anger.

You know whether you have expressed yourself appropriately by the results. Perhaps you are dissatisfied with the pay your boss is giving you. Perhaps, also, you are dissatisfied with your boss as a human being. Maybe he reminds you of your father. You have a huge savings account of anger stored for your father. In reality, what type of behavior will be most productive? You may feel a blood-boiling rage, yet it might take only a simple act of self-assertion to get your raise. So it's best to save your rage for a workshop or therapist's office, and deal with your boss realistically.

Timing

The issue is closely related to the issue of appropriateness. It has to do with using your feeling to realize your goals.

It is one thing to know that you are angry, another to share this emotion with another. Sometimes, the question of when—and whether—to share anger is a tricky one.

Take the case of Sara. She has built up resentment against her mother for twenty years. Her mother is now in the hospital, possibly dying. Sara wants a successful resolution of her relationship with her mother, not the satisfaction of blowing off steam. Yet, she has a rage at unmet needs that must be acknowledged. What does Sara do?

She chooses to keep her feelings from her mother. She realizes that her own simple acknowledgement of them, to herself, is enough to reduce her own savings bank of anger.

Sara has learned about the value of timing. The most effective feeling messages we can give are delivered at the time and place of the offense. When we delay them, save them up, and attempt to deliver them later, they are often robbed of their authenticity. However, there will be times for you when this delayed delivery will be both necessary and effective. Once again, the issue is appropriateness. You ask yourself, "Can this delayed delivery bring me a closer relationship, a raise, a clearing of the air?" If so, then it is wise to go through with it.

Forgiveness

It is important that anger over a particular issue end at some time. You will know that this has happened because you will have forgiven the other person.

If you find it hard to forgive and forget, if you carry grudges after you have apparently resolved an issue, you might want to look at what you get out of hanging onto your resentment. It might be a

13

sense of moral righteousness or power. It might be a question of avoiding a sense of loss or pain.

Remember that healthy anger is self-limiting. It ends. If yours doesn't, if it keeps feeding itself, if the flame constantly flares up again, there is something wrong.

Male and Female Games

Somewhere, back in the farther reaches of your nature, you put together an act as to how to be a man or woman in this world. You may have decided that to be a man you must roar like a bull, that you must never let anyone, especially a woman, get the better of you. You may have decided that you must be a "gentleman" at all costs and never show anger to a woman, or to anyone.

As a woman, you may have decided that you can be angry with children but never with a man. You may have decided you must please your boss at all costs. You may feel that to be feminine is to be all sweetness and light. You may have learned that you can have tantrums, but that you can never effectively assert yourself.

One sign of having achieved a healthy experience of self-assertion is when your manner of expression, and the type of feeling you allow yourself, is no longer acutely tied to your gender.

Once again, the issue is appropriateness. If you have put together a pretty strong sweetness-and-light racket, and you are in a business where heavy self-assertion is the only way to get ahead, your female games may seriously hold you back in life. This is why so many of the new anger workshops are tied to the women's movement. Feminists have been noticing that women are so heavily educated to repress hostility, especially when men are around, that they cannot put the ideas of the movement into effect, especially in their everyday working lives (this subject will be covered in Chapter Seven).

Men have also been trained to play games. I once had a client, John, who was raised by two Southern aunts. He was taught to be a perfect gentleman and never to express anger, especially in the presence of women.

John grew up to be a strapping six-footer, whom no one would have believed to have a serious problem with self-assertion. He also grew up with a huge savings account of repressed rage, which he alternately drowned in alcohol or exploded in huge inappropriate tantrums. With assistance, he was able to recognize that the source of his anger was the aunts who raised him. He then had no need to drink, and no need to explode.

How Do I Get There from Here?

Growth work in anger and self-assertion has become an important new dimension in psychotherapy. You've probably read about assertion-training, feminist anger workshops, fight-training, fear of rejection workshops, and the like. You might be asking yourself, "What's in all this for me? How can I find out more before I invest a whole lot of money?" This book will answer your questions.

Chapter Two

Anger and Happiness

You can't be happy if you can't get angry. This emotion is as basic as love, loneliness, fear, or joy. Newborn babies scream with rage when their needs aren't met. You express rage too, though you may not know it. Since it is not socially acceptable for adults to scream, you probably express rage in other indirect ways. Your body has many ways of crying out.

But it is not necessary for you to endanger your life, your health, or your happiness with outmoded ways of asserting yourself. Modern psychology has come up with new, enjoyable, exciting ways for you to get in on the *fun* of getting angry. If you express yourself in indirect, or covert, ways, this is the book for you. Look at the covert anger checklist which follows. Mark the items that apply to you. Answer honestly. This is only a partial listing—so add any other covert signals that apply specifically to you.

Keep your own signals in mind as you read this book.

You will be reading about batacca fighting, assertion training, rejection workshops, bionergetics, and other forms of growth-work. The checklist will keep you in touch with your own needs, and, in time, help you choose the form of work which is best for you.

Covert Anger Checklist

> Alcohol abuse
> Anxiety
> Blocked creativity
> Cigarette smoking
> Depression
> Drug abuse
> Excessive crying
> Excessive exercising
> Excessive sex
> Fatigue
> Fear of rejection
> High blood pressure
> Inability to say "no"
> Insomnia
> Nailbiting
> Nervousness
> Obsessive thoughts
> Overeating
> Overworking
> Phobias
> Reckless driving

Sexual problems
Tantrums
Undereating

Now jot down any other indirect ways of your own.

Anger, Aggression, and Self-Assertion

These three words are often used interchangeably, creating confusion by suggesting anger involves destruction or cruelty, as aggression may (or may not). Actually, destruction and cruelty come from incompletely expressed anger. The fear of one's own destruction and cruelty is one of the biggest blocks to the healthy expression of anger.

Webster's New Collegiate Dictionary defines anger as "emotional excitement induced by intense displeasure."

What is assertion, or self-assertion? According to *Webster's,* it is "to state or declare positively and often forcefully or aggressively." A second definition, which will become significant later, is "to demonstrate the existence of." Interestingly, the example given is "the existence of manhood." Another definition, which will also have significance later, is "To state or put forward positively, usually in anticipation of or in the face of denial or objection."

What is aggression? Once again, according to *Webster's*: "a forceful action or procedure (as an unprovoked attack) especially when intended to dominate or master. 2. the practice of making attacks or encroachments, especially unprovoked violation by one country of the territorial integrity of another, 3. hostile, injurious, or destructive behavior or outlook, *especially when caused by frustration.*" (Italics added.)

Part of the definition of aggressive is: "marked by combative readiness, marked by forceful driving energy or initiative, marked by obtrusive energy." The words "aggression" and "assertion" share the definition: "conspicuously or obtrusively active or energetic."

Note that anger means "emotional excitement induced by intense displeasure." The definition names a reaction; it carries no judgments, evaluations, predictions of destruction or pain; no predictions of loss of control or madness. It simply names your reaction to intense displeasure. We have other words—"ire," "fury," "wrath," and "indignation"—to convey loss of control, righteousness, predictions of destruction or pain.

Nor does the definition of self-assertion predict destruction or pain, though it does suggest the anticipation of denial or objection. Self-assertion involves positive energy moving outward. The self-assertion work that will be discussed later on in this book will be valuable for those of you who have difficulty dealing with waiters, salespersons, taxi-cab drivers, employers, and others who may object to the outward flow of your energy.

Aggression refers to forceful action or procedures; forceful energy, initiative, obtrusive energy. There may be destructive or hostile components in aggression. Aggression may be a result of the frustration of natural, healthy anger and self-assertion.

Hostility, Destruction, and Cruelty

According to *Webster's,* the word "hostile" means "of or relating to an enemy, marked by overt antagonism, opposition in principle." Hostility is also a synonym for an act of warfare.

To destroy means "to ruin the structure, organic existence, or condition of." It also means "to put out of existence: kill," and "to subject to a crushing defeat."

To be cruel is to be "disposed to inflict pain or suffering: devoid of humane feelings."

Compare these words—hostility, destruction, and cruelty—to the three *As*—anger, assertion, and aggression. Notice that hostility, destruction and cruelty all involve anti-life activity. Anger, aggression, and assertion involve positive energy moving outward. Destruction (the desire to kill), hostility (the need to see others as enemies), cruelty (the need to cause others pain and suffering), and the kind of aggression that involves repeated incursions into the territory of others are perversions of anger, self-assertion, and most forms of aggression.

Pleasure and Pain

The inability to express anger is involved with

the inability to experience pleasure. The word "emotion" implies a movement of energy outward. This movement of energy is a result of pleasure or pain.

The newborn infant does not experience love, hate, anger, or fear, as we know it. He experiences pleasure or pain. Once he develops an expectation that needs will not be met when he wants them to be, the infant will begin to manifest anger.

As most children develop, their expression of hostility is thwarted in one way or another. The child may be told expressing or even feeling anger is "not nice," that it is "not manly or womanly." Some children, particularly those who have been spanked, develop physical fear of their parents.

And when one form of the outward flow of emotion is blocked, all other forms are distorted in some way. Thus if the expression of pain is blocked, so will the expression of pleasure.

Imagine the last time you were furious with your husband, wife, date, or mate—and didn't express it. Chances are you went around thinking: "Look what that s.o.b. did to me! I'll show him!" I would be willing to bet you didn't have a whole lot of fun that day.

Aggression and Survival

Anger is one of the "emergency" emotions. When experiencing it, muscular excitement occurs in the back of the body, mobilizing powerful means of attack. The main organs of assault are located in the

22

upper and front end of the body, because this end is directly connected with the search for and seizure of food.

You feel anger as an upward surge of excitement along the back of the body and into the head and arms. This surge of feeling is associated with a strong flow of blood to these parts, which accounts for the fact that some people literally see red when they become enraged. If inhibitions and tensions exist which block this feeling, tension headaches often result. If a child is not allowed to express anger, he may come to feel he does not have a right to live; the right to express anger is closely associated with survival.

Aggression is associated with survival of the species, as well as the survival of the individual. Anthropologists claim that aggressive impulses have been bred into man for eons; that it is futile to pretend that these impulses do not exist.

Chapter Three

Your Furious Body

You know you're angry when you want to fight. Your whole system screams this message. Your breathing speeds up; your heart beats faster; your muscles contract. You become tense. You may actually experience a sensation of heat. Whether verbal or physically combative, or simply pacing up and down, our bodies need to do something. The fact that very often we *don't* do something physical, that we are trained from birth to repress anger, has tremendous ramifications for our bodies.

How the Fight Reflex Is Sabotaged in Children

At birth, you were deprived of a warm, comfortable environment, where all of your needs were met automatically. When you were expelled from this place of bliss, your first reaction was displeasure. You were cold and wet, probably spanked. Most likely, you had to wait more than one split second for your first meal.

Even after birth, however, you needed to be concerned only with your own wishes, satisfying your own needs, getting rid of anything that causes discomfort—a pin sticking you, a cold, wet, or full diaper. Though life was no longer the bliss it was in the womb, there were few problems. Your mother anticipated and satisfied most of your needs. You were fed, if not on demand, then on a regular schedule. When your diaper was changed, and this happened fairly regularly, you were cuddled and fondled. Without asking, you were dressed appropriately for the weather. Nothing was required of you in return.

Weaning

Once your mother got tired of providing you with this state of near bliss, trouble started. First, she wanted to wean you. She expected you to drink from a bottle; later from a glass. These objects are not warm and soft like mother; they are hard and cold. And later, you were even expected to feed yourself. At first, you demonstrated anger. You threw your bottle down, refused to feed yourself, cried. Soon, however, you learned who had the upper hand. Your mother could let you cry for hours; she could spank you if you didn't behave. She could withdraw love and affection. As an infant or small child, you learned it was worthwhile to please mother. You began to realize your own helplessness; you learned that it pays to conceal your anger.

Toilet Training

Another big demand is that you learn to control your bowels. It was easier and much more fun for you to eliminate whenever the urge arose. Your mother seemed pleased, patted you as she changed you, and hugged and kissed you afterward. Then her attitude changed. Suddenly. She began to indicate that when you have to eliminate, you should do it in the toilet. And if this weren't bad enough, if there were no toilet handy, you were expected to wait until you got to one.

This was frustrating on two counts. You were expected to tolerate the extreme discomfort of bowel and bladder; also, you had to tolerate your mother's anger if your control failed. You definitely didn't like the situation, and you couldn't show your own anger; you were, once again, too small, too helpless.

Your mother was not the only one who disapproved of uncontrolled elimination. Your peers also knew that you had to "grow up." No one can be meaner than a small child when another child has an "accident." Children cannot let their anger out at their parents, and so another child, who may be more vulnerable, becomes the target. This results, for many people, in a fear of public humiliation, which seriously impairs their expression of anger, self-assertion, and aggression for years to come.

Soon you discovered that your mother's love did not belong to you alone. When you discovered that you had to share your mother with a number of other people—baby brother, daddy, and others—a whole new series of distortions in your ability to express anger freely were added to your repertoire.

Your reaction to the arrival of a new brother or sister demonstrates this most clearly. You may have begun to act more like a baby yourself. Perhaps you were already toilet trained, and you started soiling again. Perhaps you were weaned, and you wanted your bottle back. You might have stopped sucking your thumb, and begun doing so again.

Mothers express surprise when their older children engage in covertly hostile behavior toward a new baby: "Peter seems to love little Gail, yet sometimes I could swear he holds her awkwardly, almost dropping her on purpose."

There are two reasons for this kind of behavior. One is ambivalence—we can love and hate at the same time. Another is what therapists call reaction formation. We may act very sweet and loving at a time when we feel antagonism. This happens when we want to deny anger.

Sharing Mother's Love with Daddy

When you were four or five years old, you had to deal with another step in the process of frustration.

You began to experience sexual feelings toward the parent of the opposite sex. As a little boy, you wanted to be close to your mother; perhaps embarrassingly close at times. You wanted to push your father away, but if you did so too aggressively, he got angry. You were walking a fine line, afraid of provoking your father, and so you developed a lot of repressed anger of your own.

Sharing Daddy's Love with Mother

As a little girl, your situation was complicated. You continued to love your mother, but you began to want your father all to yourself. Your cuddling may at times have been too much for your daddy's comfort. For you, as well as for your brother, the way in which you resolved this conflict set a pattern for the way you resolve other conflicts in life.

Anger and Puberty

Until puberty, your emotional life was fairly quiet. You most likely repressed your sexual desires; you had not yet encountered serious peer competition; you did not yet have the need to rebel against authority; no large demands were being made on you to take responsibility for your life.

Once you entered puberty, you had to deal with impulses difficult to control; there was tremendous competition between you and your peers; you wanted to rebel against the authorities who told you to control your impulses and to take responsibility for your life. You were frightened of and angry at all of these changes. So you developed more ways of disguising your feelings.

The Social Value of Frustration

"But what's wrong with all this frustration?" you may ask. "Should children be breast-and bottle-fed forever? For how long should they be allowed to soil their clothes? Do we want parents and children engaged in sexual activities? Do we want teenagers acting out all over the place?!" The answer, of course, is no, we do not want these things to happen.

The ability to deal with frustration is a very important social tool; the problem is that most of us do not resolve our early childhood conflicts in a way that allows us to meet adult conflicts successfully. We establish patterns that are counterproductive. We may bottle anger up and explode in temper tantrums, we may totally supress anger and play a "sweetness-and-light" game; we may try to dominate others; we may become afraid to assert outselves.

Should we blame our parents? No! Parent-blame is the ultimate loser game in psychology. It does not enable us to modify our behavior in the present; it does not enable us to break free of childhood patterns. Besides, our parents had parents who taught them inappropriate games, and their parents had parents too. The idea is to understand—without blame—where our parents went wrong in assisting us with our development, and what we, as adults, can do for ourselves in the present and for our children in the future.

Your Body's Rages

You are an extremely complex emotional organism, and the way in which you cope with your emotions is probably what separates you most widely from the rest of the animal kingdom. Your greatest pleasures in life come from the realistic fulfillment of your emotional drives. If your emotional drives are mishandled, you will not only become unhappy, but your bodily functions will be disturbed.

Because anger is the emotion which seems to demand the greatest amount of physical release, its repression can cause the greatest harm. (There are numerous organic causes for illness. This chapter should not be taken as a suggestion that you attempt to diagnose and treat your own illnesses. Consult a medical doctor about any physical symptoms you might have.)

Anger and Energy

Think of anger as a form of energy. If it is repressed, it must come out somewhere. If a sufficient amount is stored, it can affect body and mind adversely. And when we store anger, we can't control it; it may take us by surprise, attacking any part of body and mind. The task of the medical doctor, the psychologist, the psychiatrist, and any other person concerned with either health or personal growth and development, is to enable you to understand the laws governing the use of this energy. If you misuse it, you will endanger your life and your health.

Your Nervous System

There are two nervous systems which regulate the processes of the human body. The parasympathetic system maintains such everyday activities as digestion of food and any recuperative processes that are needed. The other, the sympathetic nervous system, is the emergency system, which mobilizes those forces necessary to meet a sudden demand. You react to emergencies in one of two ways—fight or flight. Both place tremendous stress on your body.

The sympathetic nervous system, which governs the fight or flight mechanism, is primitive. It evolved when man was still running from or hunting wild animals. Then, if a person did not react quickly enough, he did not survive. Today, in spite of the fact that there are very few wild beasts stalking us, our nervous systems will react in the ancient way.

When we get angry, the body gears up for action. We may be involved in a situation where the appropriate reaction is a word, such as "stop." The body will mobilize as if a full-scale fight were inevitable.

Sugar will pour into our system to make sure we have energy. More blood, containing the nutrients we need, is circulated by increasing the blood pressure and making the heart beat faster. More adrenalin is secreted, to dilate the pupils of the eyes and make us see better, and to help mobilize other needed activities. If there is no release of this build-up, as is often the case, we remain in a chronic state of preparedness, with heart beating rapidly, blood pressure up, and chemical changes in the blood.

Ultimately, the storage of all of these chemicals will cause harm.

Headache

Tension headache is a sure sign of repressed emotion. (Naturally, not all headaches are caused by tension, and you should consult a medical doctor if you have headaches frequently.) Allergies and eyestrain are often thought to be causes of headaches. These are difficult to pin down, however, and many doctors think that repressed anger is really the issue. Our language reveals the role of repression: We speak of "blowing my stack," "letting off steam," etc.

Headache is a symptom of anger turned against oneself. A client of mine, a middle-aged housewife, told me that when faced with a situation which stirs up rage, she is usually able to handle the situation calmly. The next day, however, she is certain to have a severe headache.

While she is busy, doing chores, taking care of her children, she has no problem. Once she is inactive, the headache strikes.

The tension headache is often described as a feeling of a very tight skull cap or band around the head.

The pains frequently go down the back of the neck and are sometimes attributed to muscle disease or a pinched nerve. But probably the commonest cause is muscle tension resulting from accumulated hidden anger. When we say that someone "gives me a pain in the neck," we don't mean he is pinching our cervical nerves—we mean he is displeasing us.

Anger and the Gastrointestinal Tract

"I can't stomach that man!" is a frequent expression in English.

What we usually mean by this is that a particular person makes us angry, regularly. Our language is a good indication of the way we express our emotions.

Speaking in terms of evolution, the digestive tract is the oldest system. It is therefore most commonly used as an outlet for emotions when they cannot be expressed any other way. This thirty-foot-long tube is particularly prone to expressions of repressed rage, and the manifestations of this take various forms, depending on the part of the tract involved.

Morning Sickness

The stomach can become involved in anger expression in numerous ways. Small children are known to throw up a lot when all other attempts to get their own way or assert themselves fail. Adults who "swallow" a lot of rage often throw up a lot. We are prone to say they have weak stomachs.

A peculiar manifestation of nausea is the morning sickness of the pregnant woman. There are some physiological explanations; certainly the increased estrogen in a pregnant woman's system is a factor. The pressure of the growing child on the gastrointestinal system is another.

Some psychologists attribute the pregnant woman's nausea to unconscious conflicts over whether she wants the child. A woman who is unconsciously ambivalent about her pregnancy may try to vomit out the fetus. Resentment of the responsibilities motherhood will entail can be disclosed indirectly or come out against other people. This is much more socially acceptable than anger over pregnancy.

Ulcers

You are a businessman. You have a tremendous amount of responsibility. People are depending on you. You need to keep going. You drink lots of coffee, eat light salads (to climb the corporate ladder you must stay slim), have cocktails with your meals. Soon you notice stomach cramps. You go to

34

the doctor. He says, "ulcers," clucks sympathetically, warns you about your stressful life, and prescribes a bland diet.

What has really happened? As a child, you established a certain aggressive pattern with respect to hunger and eating. It is likely that this pattern has reasserted itself in your adult life.

Perhaps you feel threatened by your responsibilities. Perhaps you want to tell someone that you are not so sure of yourself, that you don't feel you can accomplish all that is expected of you. If you are like many men in modern society, you feel you must be strong. You must project the image that you are all-powerful, that you can stand on your own two feet. Unconsciously, you want nurturing and support—and you are angry that your needs are not being fulfilled. When your body gears up to eat, blood flows to your stomach; acid is secreted. The mucous membrane which lines your stomach is unusually fragile at this time. You bleed from the tiny capillaries in the lining of your stomach; the acids literally eat away at the mucous lining. Notice that the treatment you respond to— bland foods and liquids—resembles mother's milk. You are angry that you are not getting the love and the care that you need, and your body creates a situation which enables you to get nurturing in a way that you can accept.

Colitis

You may choose to express you anger via your

lower bowel or colon. You might notice how many expletives in English include some mention of the products of the bowel. Sometimes, you may simply use these expressions. At other times, you may develop diarrhea or constipation.

This is how it works: As an infant, a bowel movement had a number of meanings for you. On the one hand, you saw it as a gift to your parents. Sometimes, however, you expressed anger with them by soiling yourself. This imposed many burdens on your parents. They had to clean you up; they might have been embarrassed if you had an accident in public. Still, this was a more acceptable and physically safer expression than breaking things or overtly expressing yourself.

As an adult, obviously you do not soil yourself. As hostility accumulates and you don't express it, it may express itself as diarrhea and cramps. You have turned your anger inward and you can seriously debilitate yourself in this way. This particular brand of colitis can cause illness and even death.

Respiratory Illness

Notice your breathing when you become angry. Does it speed up, become uneven? Repression may have serious consequences in a number of parts of the respiratory system.

Some researchers think the common cold is related to anger. You probably carry around with you at all times the viruses that cause your cold.

Why then do you get colds when you do? Is it that cold weather lowers your resistance? Is it that exposure to others with the virus causes an attack which will raise the amount of virus present so it overcomes your natural resistance? It is interesting to note that people who are having fun in the snow, even when it is very cold, do not often get sick. Yet many people report catching colds under conditions of emotional stress.

Consider the case of asthma. You may have noticed that many children hold their breath when they are angry. Once again, you must realize that from a child's point of view, such covert expressions are safer in confronting the world of adults than a simple direct statement, such as "I'm upset!" Just as a child's breath-holding is an expression of rage, so in an adult, when the anger is repressed, it will accumulate and sometimes result in an asthmatic attack. You might notice that a person in the midst of one of these attacks resembles a child in the midst of a breath-holding tantrum.

Skin Diseases

You might express your anger by attacking your own skin. One of the most common dermatological conditions is itching; in medical terminology, "pruritis." Notice that when you are angry, you are likely to speak of "itching to get your hands on someone." If you have a chronic itch, you are likely to scratch it. This leads to a secondary infection.

The technical name for this is "dermatitis factitia," or dermatitis created by the individual.

Very often anger at oneself is related to guilt. This can lead to rectal and vaginal itching, which can become extraordinarily embarrassing because it is almost uncontrollable.

Many persons we tend to think of as all sweetness and light are prone to develop hives. In childhood, these individuals often were targets of hostile actions.

One therapist quotes a patient who suffered from hives: "I was getting pushed around a lot; I had to just take what was shoved at me; I took a beating from him; he walked all over me." The only appropriate reaction is fury, but the victim of hives is under tremendous pressure to pretend that everything is all right.

The Genito-Urinary-Tract

I'm sure you have heard the expression, "piss on him!" To urinate on someone is the essence of repressed anger. Many people experience too frequent urination as a result of repressed anger. Another common expression is "hold your water!" This is used when you want someone to repress rage.

Anger is an important factor in sexual problems. A man may become impotent as a result of a desire to punish a woman. A woman may become frigid and unresponsive to punish a man.

Arthritis

"If I get my hands on that kid, I'll cripple him," you may have heard your mother say. Very often, people cripple themselves with arthritis. Some doctors relate this to repressed anger.

Strokes, Tics, and Epilepsy

You have heard the expression, "speechless with rage." This expression suggests the effect emotion has on speech, and on the entire nervous system. Repressed anger is definitely a factor in stuttering and stammering.

Strokes, tics, and such neurological diseases as multiple sclerosis have been known to be aggravated by verbal outbursts. This suggests that the repressed rage finally expressed in these outbursts is a considerable factor in these diseases.

One doctor discovered a remarkable connection between epilepsy and repressed anger. A patient known to have seizures was given an electroencephalogram to measure his brain waves. His brain waves were normal. He was then engaged in a conversation calculated to annoy him. He immediately had a seizure. The machine measured a change in his brain waves.

This is not to say that all seizures are caused by anger, only that this emotion is a major precipitating factor in a number of diseases of the nervous system.

When you are angry, you prepare for a fight with a bodily raise in the blood pressure. If you do not resolve the dangerous situations, the stress continues and the high blood pressure condition continues. The end result is a chronic state of hypertension. The problem is usually a conflict between the need to be aggressive and resolve the situation, and the need to repress the aggression, because it might be inappropriate, or out of guilt or fear. This conflict keeps your sympathetic nervous system, the one that responds to emergencies, constantly stimulated.

Notice the language as it relates to repressed anger and blood pressure. We say, "don't get your blood pressure up," and "don't get hyper."

Businessmen are especially prone to high blood pressure. One corporate executive, under phenomenal pressure from employees below him and from his board of directors above, sought medical advice regarding high blood pressure. When his doctor asked him how he felt about his business situation, he replied, "Oh, these are just the conditions of modern life." His blood pressure told a different story.

Heart Attacks

Heart attacks are often precipitated by sudden outbursts of anger that had been repressed. Of course, many calm, placid people have heart attacks. Yet when some of these patients are observed closely, it is apparent that they seldom express *any* anger at all. Extreme placidity, coupled with diseased arteries, can be disastrous.

Anger and the Mind

You are a child, your toy doesn't work; instead of asking someone to fix it, you smash it—a consequence of impaired judgment due to displaced rage. You are a teenager, upset because you are not allowed to go drinking with your friends. You run away from home. You are a young woman. You have just fought with your boyfriend. You decide to show him. You go to a bar, pick up a man, get pregnant. At all ages, anger affects our lives, our judgment, what we think, feel, and do.

Depression

One of the most serious consequences of repression is depression. When you are depressed, you are likely to do anything—from attempting suicide to overeating to biting your nails. Depression is often described as anger turned inward. We do not allow ourselves to thrust our emotion out upon the world; the energy must go somewhere; we turn it against ourselves.

Suicide

Suicide is usually a sign of anger turned against

the self. It is a major hazard in America today. While the statistics are not clear—many actual suicides are recorded as accidents—at least thirty thousand deaths a year are a result of some form of suicide.

Often the victim himself is unaware that suicide is his intention. This is especially true in the case of the reckless driver. How often have you said of someone's driving, "He is trying to kill himself?"

Eating

The digestive tract is a storage bin for repressed feelings. In addition to ulcers, colitis, and the myriad physical symptoms associated with anger, there are the emotional symptoms of overeating and self-imposed starvation.

Though they seem very far apart, these symptoms are actually similar. Some people switch symptoms; overeating for, say, six months, then starving themselves. In many, the symptoms are separate. There are stories in medical case records of teenage girls starving themselves to death, and of adults eating themselves into coronary heart disease and death. Usually, when you see someone of a normal weight who complains of symptoms related to overeating and undereating, you've found a symptom-switcher.

Overeating and undereating are related to guilt. Many people feel so guilty when they feel any anger, that they will do anything to blot out the feelings, including starving or eating themselves to death.

Sleep

You may deal with your anger by sleeping too much, or by getting involved in obsessive thoughts and creating a case of insomnia for yourself.

If you repress your feeling while you are active, thoughts about what infuriated you may enter your mind while you are trying to sleep. During the day, when you are busy, you imagine you have forgotten your rage. At night, however, when you are alone, when there is little to distract you from your true feelings, you may become obsessed with unresolved events of the day. *Ergo,* no sleep!

Insomnia is usually found in association with depression, anxiety, and guilt, all manifestations of anger turned inward. Another common reaction to these symptoms is excessive sleep.

You may sleep too much if you want to avoid the pain of your self-flagellation. Some individuals actually sleep away two-thirds of their lives, unaware that life can be joyful and worth waking up for. When persons who sleep too much are finally put in touch with their feelings the result can be very rewarding.

Drugs—Over- and Under-the-Counter Varieties

The subject of drugs may bring to mind heroin, marijuana, cocaine, and the like. But while repression is certainly a factor in the abuse of these drugs, they are not among the most serious health hazards confronting large groups of Americans today.

Rather, cigarettes, alcohol, coffee, prescribed tranquilizers and stimulants are the nation's big problems. Many abusers are turning their aggression inward.

In short, for many of us, it is a sin to express anger. And this false commandment has cost us a great deal—in terms of our health, happiness, and sense of well-being.

Chapter Four

Rages, Tantrums and Tears

"But I do say what's on my mind," Mr. Fort said, when his doctor informed him that his colitis might be related to repression. "It seems to me I am always yelling at the children, and yesterday I threw a coffee cup at my wife." What Mr. Fort is talking about is incompletely expressed anger. Your rages, tantrums, tears, and occasional incidences of violence are not indications of healthy communication. They are an indication that you are only partially letting go of what is bothering you.

There are a number of varieties of incompletely expressed anger which appear to be full expressions. Don't be fooled. If you are saying to yourself, "I don't have a problem, I tell people what I really think," or, "When I'm angry, I go to the gym and work it off or drive my car too fast, or go out and have lots of sex," you are not taking care of your anger.

You are taking care of *part* of the problem. You have recognized your body's need to do *something*. You may have chosen a physical outlet; you may have chosen a verbal one. In either case, you are releasing some of the energy created by your anger. What are you not doing? Probably, you are not telling the person with whom you are annoyed exactly what he or she did, in such a way that the person gets the point. This is very important.

In some overt games, you do tell the truth, but usually for the purpose of proving the other person wrong, rather than for the purpose of communicating something about yourself. Since most people like to be right, when you prove them wrong, they will reject your communication. Your expression of anger will be complete when you experience the satisfaction that the other person knows what's going on with you. Driving your car into a wall will not accomplish that task

You might decide to talk about your feeling. Mrs. Charles liked to do that. When her little girl Sara threw sand at a little boy at a public beach, Mrs. Charles lectured for an hour on beach etiquette. She presented her lecture in calm, measured tones. She said the words, "I'm angry," showing no feeling whatever. Sara was bored, did not listen, and returned to her play without any notion of why her mother lectured her.

46

Acting Out

You may handle anger by acting it out, performing it, even working up a hysteria. Mr. Peters, the father of a two-year-old boy, became almost hysterical when his son broke a glass dish. He worked himself into a rage. He screamed, yelled, jumped up and down. His little boy, Andrew, became frightened. He knew he had done something wrong—however, he knew little about *what* he had done wrong, or *why* his father was so upset with him.

You will know this game from a true expression of anger, because game-playing will not dissipate your rage. It will only add to the slush fund of unexpressed anger you may already have.

Your child will not benefit from this game. Even your two-year-old knows when you are being real and when you are not. Your child, and also the adults you want to communicate with, respond to your unexpressed feelings, much more than to what you actually say.

Bullying

You are likely to be a bully if you are a fearful person who won't acknowledge your fear. Bob Parker was such a person. A small man, fearful of getting into fights because of his size, he studied karate. He usually went out and picked fights with men who were no match for him, due to their lack of training. Once, he made a mistake. The man he challenged had training similar to Bob's. Bob crumpled in fear, unable to meet the challenge he himself had created.

If you are a parent, perhaps you bully your own children from time to time. You may do it with a martyrdom act (to be covered in Chapter Five). You may do it by playing the despot. Possibly, you do it by constant shouting. Whatever your game, note that your anger is not genuine; it comes from your own storage bin of unexpressed emotion.

Blasting Away

Do you blast away at people? Engage in verbal sadism? Hit below the belt? Mrs. James did. She thought she was really expressing her anger with her children when she told them how dumb she thought they were, how they would never amount to anything, how they would end up in the gutter. A small infraction, say leaving a briefcase in the living room after school, rather than putting it away, is enough to get Mrs. James going. As a consequence, her children pay no attention to her, they never know what they have done wrong, and they are very unhappy. If you asked her, Mrs. James would say she expresses anger with ease.

The blatant blaster, the sadist, is emotionally deficient. This person suffers from an almost total inability to feel on a conscious level. The purpose of the sadism is to release some unconscious feelings. Some blasters are exhibitionists; they must have an audience. Some, in the interests of preserving a kindly social image, reserve their sadism for private encounters.

Do not confuse the arrogance of a sadist for strength. These people feel very small and insignificant. Their bravado usually disintegrates once you stand up to them.

Delayed Blow-ups

Your huge blow-ups are the result of small accumulations of anger. Probably you have waited to get things off your chest. Possibly you have thought, "I'll wait until a better time," or "maybe I'm not right about this; I'll wait until I have proof," or "I'm frightened now." You may approach the big blow-up with fear. This means that you have to get yourself all worked up over it. You may have to make yourself furious before you can express yourself.

With this type of rage, there is a lot of distortion built up over the waiting period. This is not a terribly destructive expression of anger, as most relationships survive this kind of clearing of the air. Most people can accept a blow-up for what it is. But it is not the most constructive way to express yourself on a day-to-day basis.

Working It Off

You might choose to handle your anger by working it off. Usually, you are not really aware that you are working off feelings. You may feel vaguely uncomfortable, and know that you usually feel better after a workout in the gym, a bout in bed, a hard day's work. I am not talking here about the satisfaction you get from these activities; I know there are genuine satisfactions in them. Most people who use work, sex, and exercise as a dodge for feelings get little satisfaction. This is the clue to whether or not this is one of your games

Overwork

You are a wealthy businessman. You could have afforded to retire ten years ago. Yet you still put in twelve-hour days at the office, convincing yourself that your subordinates can't handle the job. Is your problem really work? No. If you did retire, your savings account of repressed fury might overwhelm you. And so you waste the years that you could enjoy, overworking to avoid your rage. Due to the socially acceptable nature of your problem, you probably won't get help unless faced with a crisis— a heart attack or your wife threatening to leave you, for instance.

The overworker often punishes people with whom he is annoyed by removing his presence—for example, from the home to the office—and working even harder. In some cases, the overworker can only experience anger in connection with work, due to an inability to handle close relationships with others. Almost always, if the overworker expresses anger, it is not directed at the person who actually offended him.

Excessive Sex

Andrea Jones thought she had found the perfect lover. He could perform for hours, make her climax umpteen times, was never tired, never unable to perform. Gradually, she became suspicious of her new lover. As their relationship progressed, he wanted to incorporate increasingly more painful activities into their "love-making." Finally, she sought help from a psychological counselor.

Andrea had found a man who used sex to work off his unconscious hostility toward women. When confronted with his sadism, John claimed his great love for women drove him to seek more and better ways of pleasing them. It became clear to Andrea that he wanted little more than a mechanical means of expressing his repressed hostility.

Many sexual athletes have a fear of impotence, frigidity, or homosexuality. They spend their lives proving they fit none of these labels. Almost all have a tremendous slush fund of unexpressed anger which keeps them from forming more gratifying relationships.

Sports and Exercise

Sometimes you hear the language of combat on the playing field. You hear a man say, "I murdered the ball," or "I damn near killed him," meaning the opponent. This language may be a sign that the speaker is using sports or exercise to work off a reservoir of unexpressed emotion.

Some overexercisers work off their aggression in single-person sports; most, however, prefer competitive sports where the competition simulates combat. Usually, a slush fund exerciser—that is, a person who takes out his repressed anger in sports or in excessive exercise—will report an irritating experience right before a strenuous workout. Also, these people sometimes have health conditions which contraindicate strenuous activity. This is an indication that self-hatred is a factor in excessive exercise.

Fast Driving

Mr. Long is very nice. He never gets angry with his wife, a woman who nags him incessantly, or his co-workers at the office. He is superhumanly patient with his children—and turns into a tiger behind the wheel of his auto. Many who are violent behind the wheel of a car have a nice-guy or nice-gal image they are afraid of losing. The anonymity of the auto protects this image.

Telling the "Truth"

"I always express my anger," Mrs. Clark says. "I always tell people exactly what I think of them." Don't be deceived by the Mrs. Clarks of this world. They only tell you the unflattering things, point out your defects, lower your self-esteem. Their truth-telling is a peculiar form of perverted anger, because they only tell you how terrible you are.

Very often, these people are liars, especially about their devotion to the truth. Once they find out that their truth-telling is not for real, however, these people make progress in therapy.

Communication

What is wrong with the forms of expressing anger covered in this chapter? Usually, no real communication takes place. If your child doesn't pick up his toys, and you call him an idiot, he doesn't know that it is his messy room that's got you going. He concludes he is an idiot, and there's nothing he can do to please you. You, on the other hand, remain frustrated because his room is still messy.

You do not need to scream; you do not need to hit. To get satisfaction from your expression of anger, you do need to communicate.

Without communicating fully, the anger remains stored in your body. You can shout at your wife and child, at your husband or boss—but if you don't feel that your communication is received, you won't settle down, you won't experience calm and resolution.

Chapter Five

The Sweetness and Light Game

All of us know someone who seldom shows emotion. Mrs. Carl is like that. Mrs. Carl also has ulcers, children who feel perpetually guilty, and a husband who drinks.

There are a wide variety of covert games. You can recognize the sweetness-and-light variety by the fact that the person playing it never seems to experience anger. This person also often projects a sense of superiority.

The Nice Guy Syndrome

Otherwise known as the "don't-make-waves-syndrome," this game involves a secret pact between you and the other guy. The pact is secret—simply because your friend doesn't know about it.

This is the pact, simply stated: "I do not allow

myself—or you—to become angry." As a "nice guy," you need to be universally liked. You feel that any self-assertion will alienate others from you; it will destroy your image of perfection; it will result in a loss of love.

Being universally liked (or loved) is considered the only way to be safe in a dangerous world. If you are angry, and you show it, the other person will retaliate.

You spend your life avoiding the imaginary retaliation of other people.

You expend an enormous amount of energy in not being yourself. And, to make it worse, this approach doesn't work. In spite of your game playing, those who like you, do; those who don't, don't. More sadly, in blocking off anger, you block the love that you really want.

The Mind-Your-Own-Business Syndrome

If this label applies to you, you believe that non-involvement will save you from emotional pain. Anger threatens your non-involvement status; if you express it, you reason, that would show you care. To reveal the extent of your caring would be to make yourself vulnerable.

Sticking your head in the sand doesn't work. Emotional investment is an inevitable consequence of living in this world. Your coldness only deprives you of the pleasures that emotional involvement can bring.

Many people who give the impression of being all sweetness and light behave that way out of a need to control. They associate anger with loss of self-control—and loss of the ability to control others.

This particular game does allow some outward expression of anger, though it is a perverse one. Usually, it occurs in conjunction with a self-righteous bullying game. It does not allow the person who is the object of your annoyance to state his case, because the controller must always be right.

Many controllers are so righteous that they are vindictive. A controller can express himself if it does not interfere with his need to be admired or even worshipped. Because he usually sees himself as right, revenge is part of his game. This person seldom shows real emotion. He expresses disapproval, from the point of view of "I'm superior, I'm right."

Suppressers

If you totally suppress your anger, you fall into one of two categories. You may be genuinely unaware of your feelings. You might typically say, "Me, I never get angry. There's nothing important enough to warrant it." You genuinely cheat yourself out of an awareness of your true state of mind. When confronted with a situation which would enrage even the saints, you are likely to say, "Yes, I can see that she is a conniving, bullying martinet who is only concerned with the amount of work she can squeeze out of us, but she doesn't affect me in the slightest." You want to be nice, to be liked, and you live in fear that you will lose the affection of the people around you if you even so much as feel your own hostility, much less show it.

The other category consists of persons aware of feeling angry. If you are this type of suppresser, you realize you have a vested interest in not showing anger. Maybe your self-image is at stake, the need to control others, or a fear of not being liked.

You control your emotions with such statements as, "So I'm annoyed, that doesn't mean I have to scream and holler at everyone." Or you might say, "I just take a sleeping pill and lie down for a few moments," or "I just go out and take a long walk and forget about it."

You place great faith in your will power if you are a conscious suppresser. You may even kid yourself into believing that you are not building up a savings account of feelings that you haven't dealt with. However, you, along with others playing sweetness-and-light games, have a store of anger which can take you by surprise in physical symptoms, sudden emotional outbursts, and possible violence.

Waiting for a Safe Time and Place

If you are like many people, you habitually put off a confrontation, hoping that a more appropriate moment will present itself. In many cases, this *is* the best way to handle a situation. You know that if you hit your husband with everything that is wrong with him the moment he comes home from work, you are not likely to communicate effectively. The test question is: How long do you delay?

If you actually do get around to expressing yourself, waiting is not a game with you. Some people, however, play the waiting game hoping that their anger will disappear. What happens then is that a tremendous contribution is made to their savings account of unexpressed emotions. Either the feeling gets twisted and distorted, or it is totally suppressed until explosion time. Either way, when it finally comes out, not very much communication is likely to happen.

What can also happen is that you get so good at this game that you forget you are angry at all. This leaves you an even greater savings account.

If you notice yourself thinking of things to say to people after a confrontation has taken place, you are likely to be a game-playing waiter. If you are in this category, these are some of the statements that are likely to be part of your inner dialogue: "Why didn't I think of that earlier?" "I didn't even feel annoyed then, but now I have a headache." "I'd like to tell him off, now!"

Displacement

If you tend to displace your anger, you do not express it at the source. Rather, you express it later, with someone or something which has little to do with your true feelings.

Clues that you are a displacer: You become suddenly furious at the slightest annoyance or minor offense; you can show anger toward your wife and kids, but not toward your boss. You attempt to put your anger off on to the least threatening thing or person.

You have an irrational fear of retaliation from the true source. You are all sweetness and light with the strong and the powerful in your life, and furious with the weak and vulnerable.

Excusing the Other Guy

"Oh, she must have had a bad day," said Mrs. James of the waitress who was rude to her. Mrs. James was making excuses for the waitress's behavior.

She experienced irritation, but made every conceivable attempt to reason or rationalize it away. If you are a diluter of feeling, your internal script goes something like this: "She must be ill, I can't possibly be upset with her." "Civilized people don't raise their voices." "I understand his point of view, therefore I can't assert myself." "He didn't really mean to hurt me."

If you are an excuser, you have to learn that it is possible to see another person's point of view—and still be angry. You may be suffering needlessly from your repressed anger, because you think expressing it requires giving up your very valuable ability to see the point of view of your opponent.

The Sweet Talker

There are some people who are always giving compliments. "How nice your dress is!" the sweet talker might say. Yet something about the compliment disturbs you. You are right to be distrustful.

You can tell by the edge of tension in the sweetness, by the saccharine tone of voice. You suspect that this person really is angry with you, and is holding back. This person is often sweetest to the one he is most furious at.

The sweet talker is often afraid to have an enemy, be it a boring neighbor he would prefer not to pass the time of day with, or a store clerk he will never see again.

Savers

If you are a saver, you carry grudges. You probably don't see yourself that way, however. Your game is to see yourself as a martyr. You may be a conscious anger-saver or an unconscious one. As a suffering martyr, you believe that you are entitled to special treatment. People are expected to anticipate your needs and wishes—after all, you do that for them. When the special treatment is not forthcoming, you accumulate even more resentments.

You end up remembering all of these imaginary injuries. You save them up, carry them around with you, complain to everyone but the person involved. You seldom deal with present hurts, but leak out slow chronic anger over past events. You get some relief, while maintaining your kindly image.

The Saboteur

If you are a saboteur, you agree to perform many services you don't want to perform—and strike back when the other person is least likely to defend against you. You might be a chronic forgetter: You agree to give your sister a ride to your mother's house—then conveniently forget all about it.

You might be chronically late. You agree to do things you don't want to do, and then keep people waiting, break appointments completely, or even arrive on the wrong day.

You might get sudden attacks of stupidity. When you don't want to fix the toilet, you don't call a plumber until you make a mess of the job yourself.

You might be sexually provocative and then frustrate the person you are flirting with.

Your game is to be agreeable, then blame the other person because you are doing something you don't want to do. All of your accidental goofs are intended as punishments, whether you are conscious of it or not. You make the other person responsible for your difficulty in asserting yourself.

Madness

The word "mad" refers to insanity and, according to common usage, to anger. This semantic ambiguity signifies a very real block to healthy communication. You may struggle to maintain an image of sweetness and light, because you equate anger with insanity and the loss of control. Actually, an excessive need for control is directly related to insanity. Who is more controlled than the catatonic schizophrenic, the person virtually unable to move, for fear he will do something wrong.

The healthy expression of anger *prevents* the build-up of toxic feelings that are so dangerous to our sanity. Many psychiatrists feel that they can assess a person's health or lack of it by the way the person reveals anger.

Do not imprison yourself in the sweetness-and-light trap out of fear of going crazy. If you become angry now and then, it does not mean that you are "going mad." You may be letting out just enough poison to keep your sanity.

Chapter Six

The Sneaky Aggressor in Your Life

Assuming you are willing to give up your own games and be up front about your anger, what should you do about the people in your life who are not where you are, who continue to subvert relationships with inauthentic games?

First, you must learn to recognize game playing in others.

The Nature of Hidden Aggression

Since aggression is socially unacceptable, we learn to mask it, allowing it to come out in a socially acceptable way. We must learn to pretend we are being helpful, agreeable. We camouflage what it is that we really want and feel. So do others, and it is easy to get sucked into their games, even after we have learned to recognize the games ourselves.

You might sense that there is hidden aggression

in a relationship if that relationship leaves you tired, drained, or confused in some way; if it reinforces bad or self-destructive habits; if there is a continual sabotage of plans. Learn to look at the results of a transaction between you and another.

Collusion

You are on a diet. You have lost fourteen pounds. Your husband brings home a box of candy and says, "Come on, honey, let's celebrate your weight loss."

You are a teenager struggling with a drug problem. You have been arrested once for stealing the money to buy drugs. Your mother leaves her purse around. It has one hundred dollars in it.

You are a young teacher on a college faculty. You've been unsuccessful in publishing. You get a lot of compliments from a teacher senior to you, who is also a close friend, about your teaching ability. Your friend doesn't suggest you write and publish, even though your future clearly depends on it.

To deal with collusion you must risk the anger of the "giver." If your husband brings home candy, he wants the temporary satisfaction of doing something "nice" for you; and, on another level of awareness, he needs to keep you fat. You must refuse the gift. In this sort of close relationship, you may also want to guide him into an examination of his motives. Perhaps you are becoming more attractive to men and he feels frightened. It is a question, for both of you, of giving up instantaneous gratification for a long-range goal. Ultimately, your relationship will benefit.

The Sickness Users

Some people always seem to be sick or getting sick, especially when you want to stand up to them.

The message in their illness is frequently, "How can you possibly be angry with sick little me." Or "Do you want to see me die young?" or "Don't say anything I don't want to hear, or I'll get sick again."

These people are seldom ever fully healthy. They seem to always have an illness in the wings to get you with. If they ever admit to feeling good, it is usually said in a way that predicts, with dread, the next illness.

As children, these people were very likely the victims of extremely authoritarian parents, the kind who never let them assert themselves. When ill, however, they found themselves to be the center of attention and concern. Only then, were they allowed to make their demands; as a result, they may have come to believe that the only way to make demands is to get sick first. Illness allows them to become dictators.

If you have such a dictator in your home or office, it will be difficult for you to defy convention and confront them. You must cope with some anger when you tell the tyrant in your life that you will not accommodate him or her any longer.

The Forgetters

The forgetter in your life cannot say no to you. Instead, he passively agrees to do what you want him to do and then forgets. The end result is that you stop counting on the person for anything. That is precisely what the forgetter in your life wants, without actually having to say anything about it.

You may be the forgetter in your life. Do you forget really important things? Do you lose your wallet or your keys? Your receipts for tax purposes? Your airplane ticket. This is aggression against yourself. You are probably not able to say to yourself, "I don't really want to do that right now!" And so you forget.

If you substitute the words, "I don't want to," for "I forget," you will get control over this sort of behavior, both in yourself, and in understanding the forgetting of others.

"But I Didn't Understand"

Chronic misunderstanding or inaccuracy is a form of hidden aggression. "I thought you wanted the report next Wednesday," a passive-aggressive subordinate might say, aborting a boss's conference. Learn to read the hidden anger messages in the goofs of people around you.

In employment especially, misunderstanding can be quite costly. Dr. George Bach, writing in *Cosmopolitan* Magazine (September, 1974), recounts the following story:

"A well-known psychiatrist in Chicago specializing in hypnosis formed a foundation and conducted periodic training seminars. To coordinate his schedule he hired a full-time office manager. On a day-to-day basis the psychiatrist was a tyrant with his staff and would particularly terrorize his office manager with last-minute rush demands. The office manager was, however, too frightened to show resentment or to offer any overt resistance."

On one occasion, the doctor decided on very short notice to hold a weekend seminar. He ordered one hundred announcements to go out that very night. The office manager, who felt abused, instead of refusing, tried to get the order out. In the process, she mistakenly transposed two numerals in the address of the seminar. This was her way of retaliating against her dictatorial boss.

You can recognize this type of mistake making because it is chronic. There is a false air of innocence when the person relays what has gone wrong. If you are an employer or supervisor, you must learn to confront this type of mistake-maker in your place of business. Once again, you must be prepared to face and deal with the direct anger that chronic misunderstanding conceals.

The Procrastinator

"Don't worry, I'll do it as soon as I can. Don't be so uptight about it!" Do you have one of these types in your life, or are you one?

How do you recognize a procrastinator? Usually,

this passive-aggressor will not be pinned down to a precise time. You know you are dealing with one of these characters when you are perpetually exasperated by delays, jobs incompletely done, and slowness. You can tell procrastination by the selectiveness of the person's snail-like pace. Usually, this person only keeps certain people waiting, and then only in certain situations. Procrastination is a form of contempt.

A good example of this is a writer who worked part time as a nursery school teacher. He was always late for school. However, when faced with an emergency book deadline, he was prompt, if not early.

Lateness

At one time, it was culturally acceptable for a man to be kept waiting by a woman. Women knew they were expected to keep men waiting, and acted accordingly.

The amount of hostility and contempt in this type of behavior was not recognized until recently, however. Individuals who are chronically late for meetings, appointments, and dinner dates are essentially saying, "See, I can keep you waiting, I'm superior." Yet this behavior suggests an underlying feeling of inferiority.

Sometimes, impotent rage is expressed by lateness and procrastination. This is often shown by workers on an assembly line, household servants, and others in subordinate positions.

Latecomers are some of the most creative apologizers and excuse-makers around. Usually, their excuses are cleverly designed to move you onto the defensive. The best way to tell hidden aggression is by its impact. If you constantly feel frustrated, humiliated, angry, and just plain put down by another person's lateness, there is hidden aggression in it.

Inability to Carry Over Learning

A woman who was married for years came to me once, complaining. "I don't know what to do about my husband. We've been together for eight years and I still have to tell him how I want my breasts stroked when we make love." It is true that you cannot expect others to read your mind. It is also true that when someone you are close to fails to come through when you express your preferences, it is a form of hostility directed at you.

If you feel forced to make the same requests over and over again, whether they refer to taking out the garbage or your sex life or whatever, you are probably the victim of the passive aggressor.

Non-learners will greet you with wide-eyed innocence when you confront them with your feelings about having to ask repeatedly. They are always ready with excuses, such as "I can't think of everything all of the time," or "If you want something, goddamn it, just tell me."

You know you are the victim by the humiliation that you feel each time you have to repeat your request. One secretary, a client of mine, told about her feelings when she had to ask her boss for her paycheck each week: "He acted as if I were asking for charity."

The Nurse

The nurse is usually found in a relationship where another person is hurting or in need. Her function (unfortunately, due to the way women are socialized, this is usually, but not always, a female anger-repression game) is to keep her victim from experiencing the consequences of his behavior.

Sometimes, the parents of a sick or disturbed child play this game. The child discovers he gets more attention when he is causing trouble. The parents must then be educated to reward or pay attention to the child when he is not ill.

The spouses of alcoholics are often in this category. Many of us know about a sweet saintly woman married to a violent drunk. What we don't always know is that the sweet, saintly woman almost totally controls her alcoholic husband.

In the case of the nurse, the issue of control is at stake. We all love to be taken care of by another when we are in need. But you must be watchful. Is your friend helping you to stand on your own two feet, or is he or she functioning in a way that helps you stay where you are? To the extent that your friend's help keeps you where you are, that friend is exerting control over you. To test the situation, see what happens when you no longer express neediness. If your friend seems upset or attempts to convince you that you are, in fact, in need, guess what? There is aggression and control involved.

Holier-Than-Thou

Moral one-upmanship does not only apply to religion. The righteous exist in almost every area of life. They get their power by constantly putting out the message, "I'm on a higher plane of development than you are."

In the world of psychology, an example could be your neighbor who has been in therapy for ten years, and who winks knowingly when you say how you feel—because she really knows. Or perhaps you have a friend who claims his current growth trip is obviously a lot better than yours.

In politics, some pacifists are so righteous that they see all others as lusters after war.

In a religious vein, these people can be Christians, yogis, vegetarians—anyone who would have you believe he is more developed spiritually than you are. It is not the fact that a person is in search of meaning in his life that marks him as a sneaky aggressor; it is the constant implication that he is morally superior to you.

If you discover, when you are with one of your "true-believing" friends, that you are constantly doubting yourself, wondering if you are concerned enough about the state of the world, wondering if you are morally fit, then you know that some kind of emotional aggression is taking place.

You can sense the hostility in this type of aggression by its impact on you. A person trying to convert you to scientology, EST, yoga, Gestalt, communism, Christian Science, or Catholicism will inadvertently betray his sense of moral superiority. If you start to notice yourself feeling just a little bit inferior, you know you've got an aggressor on your hands.

You might be tempted, in your interaction with the aggressor, to give intellectual agreement, all the while feeling emotionally resentful. Trust your resentment! When you feel something, it's your body, your mind, your emotions trying to tell you something. Don't start wondering about yourself!

You can confront the person with a remark like, "You know, your ideas sound good, but when you share them with me, I start to feel inferior; this makes me resent you. What happens then is that I give you lip-service, but secretly resent your sense of moral superiority." You may really be doing the person a favor.

Very often, we hesitate to assert ourselves out of a fear of doing harm. Tolerating some discomfort, for the sake of clearing up a relationship, may be the best thing you could do for someone. Do not get defensive with a moralist. It is the worst thing for both of you. Get immediately on the offensive and hold your ground.

Intellectualizing

How do you know when you're dealing with an

intellectualizer and not just someone who is very intelligent and knows it? The question is one of appropriateness. An intelligent person will use the gifts he has to improve the quality of his emotional life. With an intellectualizer, you always sense that your feelings are being murdered.

The intellectualizer relates to emotions with judgments. He will seldom say, "I feel angry." He will say, "You have an incestuous relationship with your father that is causing you to react negatively to me." How do you deal with this?

Once again, the first step is recognition. If you feel frozen and shut out when you try to make emotional contact with a person, you have an intellectualizer on your hands.

This person gives very little of himself to you. His aggression is expressed through detachment and by lecturing. In much the same way as the self-righteous person makes you feel morally small and doubtful, the intellectualizer makes you feel unreasonable, childish, and silly. In extreme cases, the intellectualizer may try to get you to doubt your sanity.

Some intellectualizers constantly rely on techniques to solve personal problems. One woman I counseled complained that her husband was always buying books about sex techniques. When she told him what she wanted sexually, he would quote from one of the books. Naturally, she was extremely frustrated.

As in the case of the morally superior person, you

can determine the extent of the aggression in the intellectualizing by its impact. If you always feel frustrated after contact with a particular person, there's usually aggression involved.

Trust your gut reaction to the intellectualizer—even when he or she tries to make you mistrust it (one of the intellectualizer's games). Hold your ground; trust yourself. Do not get into one-upmanship. Rather, a response like, "Cut the crap and tell me what you feel!" is most likely to break the sterile pattern.

The Non-rewarder

Some people will never give you a compliment, never say, "job well done!" They will never tell you how pretty you look, never tell you they value your opinions. This is the non-rewarder syndrome.

This person aggresses against you by instilling and fostering feelings of insecurity, anxiety, frustration. If you find yourself going to a therapist just to get some warmth, you may be married to a non-rewarder. If you find yourself constantly wondering about your job security, you may be involved with a non-rewarding employer.

What should you do? Very often, the non-rewarder is not aware of the problems others have as a result of his or her habits. You may have to do a lot of confronting with specific requests for feedback on the quality of your performance, how you look, and how the person feels about you.

The helpless person is a guilt-mongerer. He or she, and often this is a female game, puts out the message, "You're so big and strong and capable, and I'm so little and weak and vulnerable, you've got to help me."

There is tremendous power in such helplessness. Once this person has found a victim, she asserts herself with tears, weakness, and vulnerability.

If you feel drained and overwhelmed, chances are someone in your life is playing the helpless game. This is a potent form of exploitation and manipulation. You feel trapped by guilt. How do you deal with the situation?

First, take a good look at yourself? What are *you* getting out of the game? Do you need constant reassurance as to your strength and worthiness? The helpless person uses a kind of flattery. After all, in the message "I'm helpless" is the corollary— "How big and strong and together you are."

Be cautious around anyone who arouses your protective instincts, around whom you want to take over and do everything. The helpless person is usually enormously appealing.

If you are not sure whether or not you are dealing with a game-player, but you think you are, try this: The next time you suspect that the racket is being run on you, say, "I don't believe you." Tell the person how strong she really is and how effectively she is manipulating you. The reaction from a player of

the helpless game will either be a tantrum or stony
silence.

Doubt Fosterers

When you are most vulnerable, the doubt
fosterer will strike. When you are most in need of
reassurance, the doubter stirs your anxiety.

Did you just get accepted to the college of your
choice? The doubt fosterer will tell you that college
degrees are worthless. Did you just begin a new
business? The doubt-maker will tell you that you
didn't live through the depression, you don't know
that anything can happen, you should get a secure
job with the government.

A doubt mongerer sees the world in consistently
negative terms. If you feel constantly anxious in
your dealings with someone, chances are you are
dealing with a doubt-fosterer.

Doubters poison the atmosphere. Generally, they
feel inadequate themselves. Their only way of feeling good about themselves is to make you wonder
about yourself. They don't want you to surpass
them in achievement. They also don't want you to
feel too successful or sure of yourself. You either
need to ignore the doubter, or to get very angry.
State the issue clearly. Tell this person that his
doubts over your decision are of no help to you.

What's Wrong with Hidden Aggression

What do you lose when you allow relationships to

continue which are based on hidden aggression? You lose healthy interaction. You find yourself constantly feeling resentment, humiliation, fear, self-doubt. You lose the nurturing potential of relationships.

You also lose control of your life. The sneaky aggressor's motivation is to control you, to control the relationship between you. You find yourself constantly fighting this subtle form of control. This drains your energy.

Most important, sneaky aggression destroys genuine involvement and communication. Gaining these is worth the discomfort that may be required in dealing with the sneaky aggressor in your life.

Chapter Seven

Anger and Self-Assertion

If you have difficulties expressing anger, it is likely that you have difficulty asserting yourself. Remember, anger was the first way you, as a child, learned to express your dislike, disagreement, frustration, displeasure. The way in which your free expression was disrupted then affects you now.

The Assertiveness-Training Movement

All over the country, men and women are learning to say "no!" to bosses, spouses and children, to stand up to waiters and cab drivers. Best-selling books are detailing your rights to self-assertion—and how to go about getting them.

The message is: A person can be taught how to get what he or she wants, with minimal harm to others. The techniques are simple and practical;

they aim at correcting your own meek behavior. You might practice repeating "no!" over and over again, until you are able able to say no to the person making demands on you. You learn to rehearse self-assertive behavior, such as asking for a raise, a date, or anything else you might want.

You might learn to delay confrontation, by asking an angry loved one to put off an argument until you're less upset.

The assertiveness-training movement became popular in 1970, when two California psychologists, Robert Alberti and Michael Emmons, published *Your Perfect Right*. The book has sold nearly one hundred thousand copies to date.

The phenomenal growth of the movement has been largely a result of the growing strength of feminism. Assertiveness training tends to be a sequel to consciousness raising.

Women tend to outnumber men in the training groups, according to Chicago psychologist Hannah Frisch. Whether or not women have more problems with anger and self-assertion than men is under debate. It seems clear that their problems are different.

Many educators report that in a class with men, women will seldom speak out. Women will seldom express disagreement when men are around. In discussion groups, women will seldom ask for clarification when confused, and will seldom elaborate their points.

"As women, we are reinforced and complimented by being non-assertive," says Karen Coburn, director of counseling at Fontbonne College in St. Louis and co-author of the recently published feminist book, *The New Assertive Woman.* Imagine a man being admired in America for being docile and self-sacrificing!

What Happens in an Assertiveness-Training Workshop

At Assertion Unlimited: Barbara Greer, a gravelly voiced secretary in her fifties learns to say "no" to a boss who demands she make coffee. An electronics salesman, Bill Hart, learns not to feel intimidated by skeptical customers. A young woman learns to refuse her boyfriend when he asks her to do his laundry. A housewife learns to return faulty merchandise.

Assertion Unlimited offers workshops in Los Angeles, as well as in several other major cities. No private counseling is offered.

In Atlanta, Georgia, training is offered at the Unitarian Church, the Jewish Community Center, and the YWCA. In San Francisco, the groups are called "*chutzpa* workshops" (*chutzpa* is the Jewish word for nerve). They are offered by a number of different organizations.

Major corporations, such as AT&T, in New York, Proctor and Gamble, in Cincinatti, and TRW Systems, in Redondo Beach, California, are running courses to teach their own staffers to stand up for their rights.

"People are generally becoming aware that they

don't really have control over their lives," says Maria del Drago, coordinator of continuing-education programs for women at the University of California Extension. "They don't want to be militant or pushy in a negative way," she adds, "and assertiveness training seems to strike the right note with them."

The fundamental philosophy behind most of the training programs is the individual's bill of rights. At Atlanta's Assertiveness Training Institute, they call it the three "Rs." They are: the right to request, the right to refuse, and the right to right a wrong.

Your Trip Through Assertiveness Training

You are a businessman. You are having difficulties in a new position, one which demands that you assert your authority over workers who were once your peers on the job. You are feeling anxious, even losing sleep. Finally, your wife talks you into enrolling in the workshop with Dr. Herbert Fensterheim. What will you do first?

Discovering Your Assertiveness Handicaps

If you are like most people, you are assertive in some areas of your life and less so in others. You may find it easy to tell your wife off, and difficult to function on the job. You may be capable of speaking your mind, but have a tendency to do so inappropriately. The first step is to discover your handicaps, your particular, unique problems.

Dr. Fensterheim's inventory is valuable, because you score it and evaluate it for yourself. This may be the first step for you on the road to assertive behavior.

First you answer a series of questions. Examples are: 1) Can you begin a conversation with a stranger? 2) Do you buy things you don't want because it is difficult to say "no" to a salesman? 3) Are you satisfied with your social life? 4) Can you criticize a friend? 5) Can you assert yourself with women? 6) Can you assert yourself with men?

Once you have answered the questions (there are twenty-three), you circle the ones which indicate difficulties. Then, you write a sentence or a series of sentences after the circled questions to explain your problems in your own words. You set your goals. Your therapist does not make the choice for you.

Discovering the Things That Intimidate You

You are given a list of things that might intimidate you. These include: tough-looking people, feeling tender, angry people, being ignored, making mistakes, a lull in conversation.

You may add to this list anything you can think of which might make you feel uncomfortable. Then, next to each item on the list, you indicate the extent to which you are bothered. Fensterheim suggests the scale: not at all, a little, much, very much.

In evaluating the items on the list, you use your reactions of the moment, rather than how you recall reacting in the past, or how you think you might react in the future. For example, if in looking at the list, you feel fear when you consider the item "tough-looking people," you put much or very much down, even if you have talked back to tough-looking people in the past.

What's the Catastrophe?

Many people avoid self-assertive behavior out of fear of an imaginary catastrophe. Yours may be a low-probability catastrophe, such as, "If I don't relinquish my parking space, the other guy will break the windows of my car," or a higher probability one to which you give a lot of significance, such as, "If I criticize my wife, she will be angry, and that will be disastrous for me."

These are rationalizations. Your first step in actually formulating your goals will be to actually pinpoint your rationalizations. You might discover that it is fear of rejection that stops you. You will then list situations in which fear of rejection comes up—for instance, in situations where you must assert authority with subordinates—and then concentrate on dealing with those situations.

Learning to Say "No"

If your subordinates intimidate you, chances are you have difficulty saying "no" to them. Learning to say "no" is an important aspect of any growth work having to do with self-assertion or anger.

Dr. Fensterheim has designed practice exercises where you write out a response to a situation, and then compare your response to the one he suggests.

For example: There is someone at your office who is always borrowing money for the coke machine. He never pays you back. He asks you again. What do you say?

Fensterheim suggests: "No. You never pay back," or "No. You already owe too much." Notice there is little explanation.

Learning to Relax

One of the results of anxiety on the job is an inability to relax. It is difficult for you to assert yourself when general anxiety dominates your mood. In a workshop led by Dr. Fensterheim, you might learn a relaxation exercise:

Step one: Estimate your tension level. On a scale of 0 to 100, with 0 meaning total lack of tension and 100 meaning complete tension, place yourself.

Step two: Dr. Fensterheim gives you a "pleasant scene" to imagine. This may be the beach, a country walk, or a scene at a lake. There should be no disturbing elements in your scene. If you are having difficulty imagining this scene, you are instructed to think of the word, "calm."

Step three: You are instructed to tighten and relax large groups of muscles. When you tighten your muscles, you become aware of how you make

84

yourself tense. You then experience your own power to relax yourself. You hold tension for about seven seconds before exploding it out.

Step four: Learn to do the exercise consistently.

Step five: You must be alone when you do the exercise.

Step six: Keep a relaxation record. Each time you do the exercise, record the level of relaxation you reach. You give yourself a sense of self-confidence as you record the increasingly lower tension levels that you achieve.

Criticisms of the Assertiveness-Training Movement

You must experience the training for yourself to get a sense of its value. Naturally, I could only include a few of the wide variety of exercises available.

Before you run right out and enroll, you should understand some of the limitations of this form of growth work.

Some critics claim that the training may be a fad, with only superficial potential for expanding your awareness. Says psychologist Richard Farson, a former Esalen president, "Generally, human beings can only be trained for unimportant things . . . You can learn to return a bad steak through assertiveness training, but training is no solution to life's problems."

Psychologist George Bach, who has been in the anger business for a long time, feels assertiveness training does not go deep enough. Bach (whose pioneering work in aggression I will discuss in Chapter Nine) believes that aggression is an integral part of human life. He teaches you to ritualize it into fair fights.

Bach says, "Assertiveness is most useful for the underdog. It's very limited because it teaches you how to say 'no' and 'I want.' " Assertiveness will not teach you to deal with anger on a deep or lasting level.

Robert Ringer, author of the best-seller, *Winning Through Intimidation*, criticizes the movement from a different standpoint. He feels it is too polite. "I don't think there is any such thing as right and wrong," he says, "good is what I do and bad is what you do." Ringer is a real-estate salesman. His book, rejected by ten publishers, has sold 165,000 hardcover copies.

Many psychologists and psychiatrists are disturbed by Ringer's view, and by the notion that the self-assertion movement might come to reflect such views, rather than concern itself with the expansion of human potential.

"It's a new name for an old approach," says Bruce Danto, a Detroit psychologist. He calls it, "how to be a dictator and rule the whole block." Danto predicts a new series of books on how to deal with all of the intimidating personalities created by the self-assertion movement.

The most serious criticism is that training does not maximize your ability to have genuine relationships. It can give you valuable techniques and strategies in the art of everyday wheeling and dealing. For your close relationships, however, you will probably want a program that goes deeper.

Chapter Eight

Anger, Assertion, and Sex

When Charlie was very young, he thought that the word "fuck" was something grown-ups said when they were upset. It was only when he was eleven or twelve that he discovered the word referred to sexual intercourse. The words we use to express anger demonstrate the connection between this feeling and sex in our culture.

A child, overhearing his parent's lovemaking, may assume some harm is being done. He also experiences some excitement as he discovers what they are really doing. The connection is established.

Aggression has a positive function in the human mating game. The little boy and girl who tease each other into a physical fight are expressing their sexuality. This is carried over into adulthood when women deliberately irritate men into physical contact, as a form of sexual invitation. Or when adult men deliberately establish physical contact with a woman in order to make an advance.

Aggression in the Sexual Act

Fights between husbands and wives often end in coitus. This is common in humans and in animals.

Even so simple an expression of sexuality as kissing can contain hostile components. These can range from nipping and biting to forcing the tongue into the partner's mouth.

During sexual foreplay, potentially painful acts, such as biting, squeezing, and pinching are often engaged in. These are often found stimulating.

This behavior is often found in animals as well as humans.

Sadism and Masochism

This is the area where aggression goes over the line and becomes cruelty. Freud believed that cruelty and sex were, by the nature of sex in civilization, inextricably intermingled. Many modern therapists would argue that cruelty, in any area of life, is a function of repressed natural aggression.

Sadism, which is overt sexual cruelty, and masochism, which is the derivation of pleasure from being the recipient of such cruelty, are only the most obvious ways in which human aggression finds its way into the sex act. Rape is another clear cut way that aggression becomes sexual.

A doctor reported a case where a man, whenever he was angry, took his wife's diaphragm out of a drawer, threw it at her, insisted she put it in, and proceeded to have sexual intercourse with her.

Legally, this is not considered rape in most states; it is a husband's legal right to have sexual intercourse with his wife. However, it is sexual activity under duress and it illustrates the presence of aggression in human sexual activity.

Some rapists are only able to perform sexually when they are violent with a woman. These men may attack a woman physically, or make her perform humiliating acts, such as crawling or dancing for them.

Sometimes knives or guns are involved. To a disturbed mind, manliness may be associated with violence.

To demonstrate the complexity of this issue, I will describe an incident told to me by a woman I counseled. A man held a gun to her, and threatened to rape her. She began to help him off with his trousers. Once he sensed her apparent willingness, he lost his erection. He broke down totally after this failure, and had to be hospitalized. (This is not a recommendation that you deal with a rapist this way, as the psychology of rape is enormously complex.)

Sexual gratification is seldom the primary factor in rape. Rape is usually an expression of rage against women.

Some men can only perform sexually when they are angry at a woman, or when they think she is inferior or unworthy. These men are only successful with prostitutes, in a rape situation, or with a woman whose social class they see as beneath their own.

Impotence

Another male anger game that expresses itself sexually is impotence. Though fear may be a component in impotence, I have often found that hostility, and the desire to frustrate, are significant components.

With one couple I counseled, the woman's frequent need for sex, and the man's inability to perform, was a source of agony for both of them. I asked the man to complete this sentence: "If I could tell you how angry I am, I would say . . . "

He expressed many long-repressed feelings— anger that his wife was unlike his mother, that she worked and had a career, that his dinner was never ready on time.

The wife just listened. Her husband had never felt free to express his feelings because he also had a great deal of respect for her and was in conflict between two sets of values.

Once the husband could accept his feelings, the sexual problems caused by repression were on their way to clearing up.

Female Sexual Anger

Women have different ways than men of using sex to express anger. This is not because women do not need sex, do not have sexual urges equal to or more powerful than those of men. It is because men and women are socialized to be very different from one another.

Men learn to be active, women to be passive. More male games are overtly hostile. This is especially true in the case of rape. Some male games are passively aggressive, such as impotence.

Some female games appear to be overly aggressive—teasing, promiscuity, using sex to get favors, having extramarital affairs. In fact, they are a function of *misplaced* aggression.

Promiscuity

Promiscuity suggests a need to prove oneself lovable. Some doctors feel it is rebellion against the person, usually the woman's father, who originally made her feel unlovable. "Say you love me," the nymphomaniac almost invariably says to her lover of one night. She does not get much physical gratification from sex, but is engaged in a hopeless search for love.

Young women sometimes demonstrate rage toward rigid parents through promiscuous sexual behavior. Caroline is a case in point. She loved her father deeply and was competitive with her mother.

When she was twelve, her father left. She blamed her mother for this. Shortly after, she began to have sexual relations with various boys at school. At thirteen, she was pregnant and came into the clinic for abortion counseling. It was difficult for her, but eventually she came to realize the degree to which her behavior was aimed at punishing her mother.

Teasing

Teasing is a hostile act on the part of many women. One woman I counseled used to say, "I know there is no real love possible between men and women, so I might as well get what I can materially."

The suggestion of sexual activity, never intended to be given, is frustrating to men, and the tease knows it. Sometimes, the tease is conscious of her actions; more often than not, she is unaware of what she is doing.

For some women, teasing is an attempt to gain control over men. Many women resent the submissive position society and men demand of them. They use covert ways of gaining control.

Men often feel angry when they know they are being teased. (Sometimes, they will falsely accuse a woman of being a tease just to make her feel guilty.)

The extreme of teasing is when a woman provokes a man into raping her, so that she can make him feel guilty, or have a serious punishment inflicted on him.

Prostitution

We talked earlier about women who use sex to get money and material things from men. Many women still do not regard sex as essential to their own well-being, but as a favor they grant the men in their lives. They are chiefly concerned with getting the act over with.

Many prostitutes are openly disparaging of the men they deal with. One man I know, a man who for many years was unable to function sexually due to a conviction that his penis was too small, finally got up the courage to go to a prostitute. When he undressed, she took one look at him and said sarcastically, "You must have been behind the door when they handed dicks out." He felt devastated.

The Strip-Tease Artist

She is a combination of tease and prostitute. She excites men and does not deliver, yet she gets paid. It would seem that she has the best of both worlds. Yet she has the same condescending attitude toward men as the prostitute, and the same, generally unsatisfying, sex life.

The Extramarital Affair

This is a game played by both sexes, but there are variations common to each. All forms of the game involve anger.

A woman often has an affair for the sake of reassurance. Commonly, men are not verbally affectionate enough for most women. A woman will show her anger at her husband by having an affair. The act says, "I'll show him." That she wants to "show" her husband is usually manifested by the fact that she makes sure he finds out, though it may appear that she is doing her utmost to conceal the act.

A man is likely to indulge in affairs for the purpose of proving his "manliness." Sometimes he is angry because his wife refuses him sexually, or doesn't climax, or doesn't particularly enjoy sex. He may see this as a reflection on himself, rather than as simply something that is going on with his wife.

Sometimes a man is more potent with a girlfriend than with his wife. This is usually a result of a pile-up of petty irritations that accrue in the course of everyday living. If these remain unexpressed, they will interfere with sexual pleasure.

Some men believe they must have a perpetual source of sexual gratification, especially when their wives are unavailable; for example, during pregnancy or on a long trip. Some men rationalize that they will become ill if they are not always sexually gratified. You know that anger is a component when the man conveniently lets his wife find out.

Sexual Dysfunction

Difficulties in actual sexual performance include the inability to have erections, ejaculations, orgasms. Anger is often a factor. Reactions to sexual frustration include depression, poor self-esteem, and anger. Anger can be both cause and effect in this area.

The Frustration Game

Both men and women can use sexual frustration as a weapon. Men are vulnerable in the area of their sexual skills. To suggest to a man that he does not perform well hurts him to the core. This can make him extremely hostile.

For women, belittling of sexual skill is not that traumatic. In our culture, a woman's greatest vulnerability is in the area of her lovemaking. A sexual refusal frustrates her mainly because it takes away proof of her lovability. This is not to say that women don't have strong sex drives; they do. But psychologically, women have a strong need to be loved, and when this need is frustrated, there is tremendous sexual anger. In short, the greatest source of frustration for a woman is to feel she is not lovable; for a man, it is to feel he is not sexually skilled.

Sexual Variation

Though it is generally agreed that most forms of sexual behavior are acceptable, when agreed on and enjoyed by both partners, some people feel belittled or degraded by certain activities.

If one partner believes that any of the sexual

variations are wrong, or animal-like, or requested for the purpose of humiliation, a great deal of resentment is likely to be the result.

Some people do inadvertently convey hostility toward the opposite sex in the way that they request a particular variation.

Loneliness

Frequently, sexual hostility is related to a sense of alienation. This is especially true among young people. Loneliness and alienation stem from a conviction that no love is possible. I have heard this over and over again from young people. This type of rejection is overwhelming to many. In reaction to it, young men and women are angry.

What they often do, in response to this anger and growing sense of alienation, is seek closeness wherever they can find it. In the sex act, you are as physically close to another as you can be. This closeness may or may not be emotionally genuine or longlasting. However, in most cases no real bond is established, when the drive is a loneliness that is excessive.

Aggression and Sexual Pleasure

Aggression can be a source of sexual pleasure when used in moderation. Most important is to recognize anger when you are experiencing it, and to use it in your relationship—rather than letting it ruin your relationship.

Chapter Nine

Fighting for Intimacy

Suppose someone told you you had to fight to love. I mean really fight—hit people, insult them, call them names, blow up at them, complain about everything under the sun. Suppose someone told you that doing all of these things would facilitate intimacy on the job as well as in the home. Dr. George Bach, author of *Pairing, The Intimate Enemy,* and *Creative Aggression,* feels that constructive aggressive rituals can improve the quality of your life and make it easier for you to be with others.

Bach maintains that we lose our spontaneity to the extent that we control our aggressive impulses. Many of our social rituals, from the big "hello" with which we greet each other, to the handshake, to the office party, to the retirement party, are designed to encourage us to control our impulses.

"The buildup of closeness, intimacy, or any

interpersonal reality demands the sharing of other than 'friendly' feelings," says Bach. Relationships remain impersonal and you do not proceed to intimacy unless you can also express negative feelings.

"The reality of getting close to someone else means that there will also be an inevitable build-up of personal reservations, doubts, anxieties, and negative value judgments about people we first meet." If you must always worry about your social acceptability when you communicate these feelings, you will not communicate fully. This is why Bach advocates socially acceptable aggression rituals.

Most of us are educated to claim we have "nice" feelings when we don't really have them, or when they are mixed with negative, angry, aggressive feelings. Consider five-year-old Allan: His mother just gave birth, and his father is attempting to prepare him for the new baby's arrival home.

"Aren't you happy about your new baby sister?" Allan's father says. Allan may want to say, "Yes and I'm also scared and angry about losing my monopoly on you and Mommy." Allan probably knows that this answer will not be acceptable to his father. So he says words to the effect that he is very happy about the new baby. Everyone is surprised when Allan sneaks pinches and makes the baby cry.

Most of us sneak our pinches. We make those around us cry silently. Bach's purpose in designing aggression rituals is to have us get our pinches out in the open, where we and the people in our lives can deal with them.

The Theory of Constructive Aggression

Your release of aggression is constructive to the extent that it is informative and has impact. It is destructive to the extent that it only expresses hurtful hostility.

Each has designed rituals which increase informative impact and "facilitate the safe release of irrational, free-floating, intense underlying anger that creates destructive aggressive interaction."

Only one of these rituals is intended to facilitate specific behavior changes. This is the "fair fight for change," and we will take it up last.

In Bach's aggression-training workshops, there is laughter as well as insult, childlike fun as well as frighteningly intense communication of material that has not often been communicated by the individual involved.

Says Bach, "All (of these communications) are not only permitted but encouraged. The so-called disordered, inappropriate, and out-of-line communications are both appropriate and constructive within the context of the aggression rituals."

Instead of driving people apart, the rituals can bring them together, if practiced in a safe environment.

The "Vesuvius"

How can a screaming release of pent-up rage make you and another person more intimate? You play according to the rules, for one thing. You only engage in what is called a "vesuvius" with the permission of the person with whom you are angry! That person agrees to sit quietly, listen, and not respond.

How do you use the "vesuvius"? In a family setting, a time may be set aside each day for each family member to vent his or her resentments. In a work setting, a vesuvius meeting can replace a ten o'clock coffee break. Many workers report feeling much more energetic after such a meeting than after coffee and doughnuts.

Bach suggests you use the "vesuvius" in connection with happy events, too. If you are getting married, you know how to express your happy feelings. But what about your fears and hurts and angers? What about your doubts? Your marriage might benefit from a clearing of the air ahead of time.

This clearing of the air eliminates the need for brooding disputes over minor issues.

The "Virginia Woolf"

"The 'Virginia Woolf' is a free-for-all, no-verbal-holds-barred, below-the-belt-line insult exchange between two people." You usually set a limited time period, such as two minutes. This ritual provides you with a structured way to get out the kinds of resentments that fester over periods of time and ultimately destroy relationships.

1. Mutual consent.
2. An agreement of absolutely no physical violence.
3. A commitment to treat the exchange as "off-the-record." This is especially important, as the participants have to feel secure enough to express below-the-belt insults.
4. A time limit.

You scream as loud as you can in the time period allowed. You concentrate on your own attack and do not attempt to listen or respond to what your partner is saying. If you are successful, you will have used gross exaggeration, abuse, body expression, and sarcasm.

Bach feels that the ability to tolerate a "Woolf" is a measure of intimacy.

The "Haircut"

This is adopted from a Synanon technique. You get to scold a person close to you for a specific offending behavior. You must limit yourself to this behavior and you must have his consent. The result is that you get a catharsis over a specific hurt.

The offender may request clarification, but he may not respond to the "haircut" itself. Once the offender recognizes what he has done, he may ask for a "doghouse release." This is a penance which the initiator of the "haircut" administers, and which then obligates him to forget the offense. The person receiving the scolding may not wish to acknowledge responsibility, or may simply reject the "haircut." In that case, the ritual is ended.

The Batacca Fight

Here you get to release your anger physically, using a foam bat. Since you can't hurt anyone with such a bat, you are free to swing with total abandon. You get the physical expression of anger, without harming the other person. This ritual allows people who are a poor match in strength to fight without fear. The rules:

1. Mutual consent.
2. Handicapping when huge differences in size occur.
3. Agreement on parts of the body not to be hit.
4. Time-out zones.
5. Time limit.

In a batacca fight you can release your anger with a tremendous sense of play and spontaneity. This takes the fear out of getting angry.

The Batacca Lashing

This is a "haircut" administered physically: "It is a mutually agreed upon spanking in which the offender allows the offended person to physically release his feelings of hostility over a wrong-doing." It is usually the offender who requests the batacca lashing as a kind of "doghouse release."

Sometimes, the offender is not available. Very often, extremely intense anger surfaces in connection with death or divorce. In that case, a sack or pillow can be used to represent the offender who is then lashed in effigy.

The "Slave Market"

Here you get to experience total domination or total submission. With a partner you decide who is to play which role first. The slave then sets limits— for instance, "I won't sing." Once the ritual has actually begun, however, the slave is committed to doing as he or she is told.

The master then orders the slave to do something which that person would not ordinarily do—for example, a passive, shy person might be ordered to shout obscenities. This ritual is particularly valuable in places where there are definite discrepancies in power. In male-female relationships, where the man often feels pressured to take the dominant role and the female the passive one, many find that they get genuine pleasure from this kind of role reversal.

Attraction-Reservation

This involves a rotation of pleasing and unpleasing comments about your partner. The attraction-reservation ritual makes it easier to express criticism. What most people do in relationships is avoid seeing what they don't like, or else they simply withhold the information to be polite. This causes slush-fund blow-ups and impedes intimacy. Sometimes, withholding information prevents a relationship from occurring in the first place.

You get to say anything, whether superficial—"I don't like your tie"—or emotionally significant—"You really hurt me when you say . . ." Regular use of this technique helps keep your relationship fresh.

Self-Reproach

This is a great way to get rid of your self-hates. You do it alone. Standing with your eyes closed, you recall awakening in the morning. You then begin to find the things you've done which make you feel ashamed, angry with yourself, or embarrassed. You scold yourself, saying such things as "Dummy! Stupid!" When you arrive at the point where you are no longer displeased with yourself, and you begin to feel silly, you stop. Then you get to forgive yourself.

This ritual is valuable in getting rid of your backlog of self-hating memories. It may prevent depressions caused by anger turned against yourself.

Persistence-Resistance

This is an excellent self-assertion ritual. You get to persist in the face of someone else's "no," and you get to resist the demands others make.

Here's the way it works: You agree with your partner on who takes which role first. If you are in the persistence role, you make a request. Your partner agrees to say "no," and to defend his response appropriately. The ritual ends when either one of you gives up.

This can be an effective means of exploring the demands you make on others and those they make on you. Do you feel rejected when you give up too soon, without checking out the reasons for your partner's "no"? Do you give in too soon? Are you accommodating in a phony way? Try this ritual and find out!

Hurt Museums

Most people harbor secret resentments. These secrets get in the way of intimacy. What you do in the hurt museum ritual is to put your relics on display and get clear of them.

You do this by agreement with your partner. If you are in an on-going relationship, you focus on the hurts inflicted by your current partner. If you are in a new relationship, you tell about past relationships which might impede your new one. You share everything your old partner ever did to you. This makes it less likely that your new relationship will be contaminated by the old. You may also write down your hurts and exchange lists.

You have these options for dealing with the hurts:

1. Bury certain items by agreeing to forget about them.

2. Barter some items.

3. Where there is material for constructive change, agree to handle that item in the fair fight format.

4. Enshrine some items permanently in the hurt museum, because it is enjoyable to remind the other person of them.

Belt-Line Sharing

Intimacy requires respect for the sensitivities of others. To act on this respect, you need to know what these sensitivities are and you need to let your intimates know yours.

You need to realize that what is "belt-line" to you, might be minor to another, and vice versa. In this ritual, you agree to respect the other's sensitivities, even though they seem neurotic to you.

Insult Clubs

Here you get to dump your stereotyped notions about people in a safe setting. We all have prejudicial ideas, whether about Jews, Blacks, Mexicans, men, women, or children. We seldom express them openly, yet all of us slip up at times. These stereotypes are especially harmful on the job, where unspoken resentments impede people's pleasure in work.

What you do is: Each group huddles together

and gathers up an arsenal of their most primitive, irrational, and unspeakable stereotypes of the other group. Let all your negative feelings surface. Each person in both groups takes a time-limited turn tongue-lashing the others.

The value of this is that an insult-exchange, which would be tremendously anxiety producing done on an individual basis, when done in a group situation is emotionally safe and even fun. It tends to defuse the tensions caused by group differences.

The Fair Fight for Change

The fair fight for change is a special ritual for intimates. It is described in Bach's book, *The Intimate Enemy*.

Bach recommends daily fighting to keep intimate relationships up-to-date and to clear up old grudges. Spouses, lovers, family, or friends must learn to fight fairly.

Here are some of the elements:

1. Discover what your belt line is and display it honestly, so that the other has the opportunity to win your trust by not violating it. If your belt line is so high that it prevents your intimates from fighting with you, you may have to do some work to adjust that.

2. Determine and share your Achilles' heels. These strategic weak spots, often concealed through years of marriage, must come out into the open. The Achilles' heel, says Bach, is what the belt line is designed to protect.

3. Your next step is to equalize the fight. That is, you make adjustments for the power relationship in the family, adjust belt lines so that they are fair, and begin.

Fighting as Information Retrieval

"For real intimates, the process of eliciting information about a partner's feelings never ends because their relationship is forever evolving," says Bach.

If a friend reads a new book, enters therapy, takes a trip, takes a new lover, buys a new car, makes more or less money, his or her feelings are evolving. As a concerned intimate, you want to keep up to date. Asking is one way. For fight-trained intimates, fighting is another.

Scoring the Intimate Fight

Bach has developed a method for scoring the fight. He maintains it is not necessary to master this method in order to fight constructively. Some people find it valuable; others find it plain tedious.

Nine dimensions make up the fight elements profile. They are:

1. Reality. This measures the authenticity of the fight. A fight is realistic to the extent that the fighter's aggression is based on justifiable gripes. Also, the emotions must feel real and authentic.

2. Injury. This refers to the fairness of the fight, whether it is fought above or below belt lines.

3. Involvement. This measures the seriousness of the fighter's engagement. A fight may be active or passive, reciprocal or one way.

4. Responsibility. Here you determine the degree of your "ownership" of the fight. Are you participating fully? Are you acknowledging that it is your fight?

5. Humor. This, believe it or not, is an important quality of a constructive fight. Many people do not fight because they take fighting too seriously.

6. Expression. If you are overt, and your reasons are obvious, you get a plus here. If you are covert, sneaky—if the reasons for your fighting are not obvious—you get a minus.

7. Communication. Here you rate and are rated on the degree of clarity of your communication in the fight.

8. Directness. Do you focus on your present opponent and his or her actions? Or are you talking about his mother, his kids, and what he did last week? This dimension measures the present-centeredness of the fight.

9. Specificity. Do you refer to your opponent's specific, observable behavior when you attack, or do you swing wide, theorize and psychoanalyze? You are more likely to get the changes you want if you limit your attack to specific behavior.

With your partner, you determine whether or not your fight was bonding or alienating. Did it bring you closer or did it drive you farther apart? Once this is established, you rate the effects of the fight. Here are your criteria:

1. Hurt. The score is "hurt increased," if one of you feels more damaged by the fight; "hurt decreased," if you feel less hurt after fighting, if the fighting took care of some hurt.

2. Information. Did you get new knowledge about your partner as a result of the fight? Rate your fight "new" and give yourself credit if you did. If you are fighting about "the same old things," rate your fight redundant.

3. Positional movement. How much progress have you made toward resolving your fight? Rate yourself "ground gained," if you got clarification or movement; "ground lost," if the issue has deteriorated.

4. Control. How much power do you have over your opponent's behavior as a result of this fight? (I mean by this healthy, sanctioned power.) Rate yourself "control increased" for an increase in acceptable power; "control decreased" for a loss.

5. Fear. How has your fear of the other person or of the fight situation been affected by this fight? If you feel you can drop your guard, rate yourself "fear reduced."

6. Trust. What has happened to your confidence that your partner will treat you in good faith as a result of this fight? Rate your fight "dependable," if your trust increased; "undependable," if it decreased.

7. Revenge. What has happened to old grudges as a result of this fight. Have they increased or decreased? Rate yourself "revenge forgiven," if old grudges have been cleaned up; "revenge

stimulated," if your feelings are angrier.

8. Reparation. If you and your partner are willing to take action to repair injuries, rate yourself "reparation active."

9. Centricity. This measures the amount of closeness you achieve as a result of the fight. Are you more or less important to your partner? Is he or she more or less important to you?

10. Self-Count. How is your evaluation of yourself affected? Do you like yourself better or worse?

11. Catharsis. Usually, if you have a good fight, you feel purged. This is one measure of the value of the fight. Mark yourself "released," if you have a good clean feeling after fighting; "inhibited," if you don't.

12. Cohesion-Affection. Your feeling of "optimal-distance" is the degree of closeness to your partner that you feel most comfortable with. What has happened to this as a result of your fight? Rate yourself "closer," if attraction has increased; "more distant," if it has decreased.

Creating Your Own Rituals

You can create your own aggression rituals! Bach describes rituals "mainly as transitional structures, bridging devices, and temporary supports, much like balancers on a bicycle."

"But these rituals are phony!" some of you will say. Yes, they are, Bach would probably respond, as phony as learning to defecate in the toilet.

Because most of us have not socialized our aggression, we release it in "dirty," harmful ways. A ritual gives permission to express feeling. Funerals structure grief, christenings structure joy at birth. The ritual of aggression gives you permission to express your anger, and to assure you, via controls, that it is safe to do so.

Bach's Theory of Aggression

Why do you fight? According to conventional theory, people fight to "do each other in"—in other words, to win. According to Bach, people fight "to provide each other with interest, entertainment, and stimulation, and to reduce the enormous aggression reservoir that builds up by fight avoidance instinctual propensities."

Winning is dangerous in a fight. It usually means you have lost intimacy.

Bach also feels that the anthropological findings of Ardrey, Lorenz, and others, that human aggression is inborn, is "theoretically interesting, but useless in answering the urgent question of how to control aggression." It is not a responsible position, psychologically speaking, to tell people that they are uncontrollably aggressive, either because of genes or the environment. These theories have become an excuse for fatalistically accepting war, sadism, and a host of lesser human cruelties.

A more useful notion, in Bach's view, is that aggression is manageable. Not only is it manageable, it is a valuable means of transmitting information and bringing about change among intimates and co-workers. What can you find out from a fight? You discover what conditions would further provoke the angry person, and maximize the hurt potential of the relationship. You also find out what will minimize it.

You discover what will bring you closer to another and what will alienate you. You find out what your "optimal distance" is, you get information about the power hierarchy in the relationship, and about your partner's loyalty, among other things. The anthropological and genetic theories see aggression as a terminal goal.

Bach sees fighting in a relationship as a process of information gathering. He acknowledges the confusion in the definition of aggression. It includes notions of hurt, as well as notions of energy and vitality.

Constructive aggression, according to Bach, is fair fighting among intimates. A result is new, authentic information about the relationship. The information is useful in these ways:

1. It lets the partner know where he or she stands.

2. It clearly states the current conflict in terms that allow for resolution.

3. It may remind partners of belt lines, "optimal distance," hierarchy.

4. Or it may re-organize the above-mentioned limits, so that they are more fair—allow for greater information exchange.

Fights are constructive to the degree that they

allow you an emotional and physical release, without harming you or your relationship. And don't forget the fringe benefits! You get to make contact, and you just might have a very good time doing it.

Chapter Ten

Releasing the Rage in Your Body

What do you do about the rage trapped in your body, rage manifesting itself as colitis, ulcers, cigarette smoking, sexual problems, and so forth? There is growth work aimed at releasing this rage, releasing repressed sexuality—and releasing your potential for joy and pleasure. There is anger and assertion growth work which allows you to attack the body directly; emotional growth takes place as a by-product of the release of blocked areas of the body.

Wilhelm Reich

One of the founders of western body work, Reich stressed the release of sexual energy. He believed that neurosis is not so much an aspect of your personality, but a set of protective mechanisms, an armor around your personality which must be broken down so that you can begin to live freely.

Your body shape tells the doctor what your armor is. It is, in other words, a representation of your mind. In Reich's view, the therapist can only reach your mind via your body.

Reich was respected by other psychiatrists in the twenties and thirties. But when he began making connections between eroticism and psychotherapy, other therapists turned against him.

He believed in a fundamental universal energy, which, if harnessed, would enable man to build civilizations. He claimed it was the blocking of this energy in man which produced psychosis, neurosis, and even such physical ailments as cancer.

In 1939, Reich claimed that through his research into the function of the orgasm, he was able to isolate the life force. He called this force the "orgone" and built "accumulators" to store and control it. He put his invention on the market, claiming it could cure physical as well as mental illnesses.

There are always many people desperate for a cure for disease. The orgone box became the rage among these people.

Reich's problems began in earnest when he tried to market his invention by mail. The FDA opposed his claims and tried to put a stop to his sales. He was sent to jail for contempt of court when he continued to use the mails to sell his invention. He died in jail in 1957.

Most therapists who call themselves Reichian
dismiss his theory of the orgone. They do give him
credit for having discovered the connection between sexual energy and the universal energy
which keeps nature in balance. They believe, like
Reich, that short circuits in sexual energy cause
human psychic problems. They emphasize more
and better orgasms, and better management of
them, much as Reich did.

They would also agree with Reich that the body
reflects the mind, that in the body's armor, and in
releasing it, lies the key to health. In the Reichian
view, sexual activity is the highest manifestation of
the body's self-expression. With orgasm as the
culmination of sex, it is the experience that most
directly connects man's outer experience to his
mind. In other words, healthy orgasm means
healthy mind.

What Happens in Reichian Therapy

The Reichian therapist first attempts to break
down your body armor. This is a means of stripping
away defenses of the mind. Then your receptive
mind is fed a balanced flow of energy through the
use of the orgasm. The theory is that the orgasm
correlates with a universal flow of energy; once you
have totally free and healthy orgasms, you will be
in tune with the universe.

You might be taught to scream, to breathe

deeply, to pound with pillows, towels, and bataccas, encouraged to vomit and defecate during treatment. This, theoretically, breaks down your muscular armor.

The therapist may begin with a deep massage, progress to masturbation, mutual masturbation, intercourse, other forms of sexual interaction and eroticism.

Always the goal is the same—to improve the quality of the orgasm. Therapy may take place in either group or individual settings.

In the words of Thomas Kiernan, author of *Shrinks, Etc.*, Reichian therapy is "the ultimate sex therapy," even though its purpose is not to cure sex problems, but to cure general neuroses. If you become interested in Reichian work, be aware that it is among the most demanding forms of therapy, both physically and emotionally.

Bioenergetics

Alexander Lowen, a student of Reich's, considers muscular tension a basic factor in neurosis, or in any difficulty in expressing emotion. He claims the body has one energy—the bioenergy—that is responsible for physical and emotional health. In bioenergetic work, feeling is released in the body in three important ways.

In the first place, the body is exposed. This enables the therapist to observe the breaking down of the armor. Men and women doing bioenergetic work wear either leotards or underwear, or strip entirely for the session.

Second, the body's energy is mobilized by learning new breathing and movement techniques. This facilitates release of feeling. The total setting supports the release of feeling which takes place during this aspect of the work.

Third, there is direct physical contact between patient and therapist as a result of this work. The desire for and fear of this contact is a major factor in all forms of therapy, according to Lowen.

"Why must the body be exposed? I would find it humiliating," you might say. Nakedness is a great leveler, stripping the individual of ego pretensions and, sometimes, ego defenses.

When a group of people are naked together in a supportive environment, according to Lowen and his followers, feelings of shame and embarrassment tend to disappear and one often experiences a sense of release and freedom.

In this setting, you get an opportunity to let go of your need to maintain appearances or to support an ego image. Once you drop your concern with appearance, you can begin to enjoy some spontaneity or joy in life.

What is the relationship between body and mind? Lowen says, " . . . the body is the person, the person is the body. We have no real existence apart from our bodies." What happens in your body is, essentially, a reflection of what goes on in your mind.

What Happens in a Bioenergetic Group?

First, your body is studied from two points of view. One is the form or shape of the body. The other is the degree of flexibility or rigidity with which you hold yourself together.

You will stand before the group. The members will look at the proportion of your body, the harmony of your musculature, your facial expression, posture, etc. They will notice whether or not you stand squarely on your feet, whether you are too thin, fat, or muscular. The group discusses the impression your body makes on them, giving you an opportunity to increase your understanding of body language.

Learning to Say "No"

It is interesting to notice that almost every form of anger or self-assertion work involves a method of learning to say "no." For most people who have difficulties in the area of anger and self-assertion, saying "no" is a problem.

Any chronically contracted muscle or rigid area of the body is, in effect, a repressed "no," according to the bioenergetic view of things. Therefore, it is important to learn to say "no" in a context which releases that rigidity.

The "no" must be stated in word and deed. In the group session, you and the other group members will take turns practicing. You might lie down on a foam mattress and strike the bed repeatedly, saying "no." You will be encouraged to use a loud, convincing tone. The group will assist you by observing and commenting on how effective your communication is.

At first, your action is not likely to be very convincing. Your blows may lack force, your voice may sound frightened, you may hesitate.

The group may assist again in a number of ways. They may cheer you on, encouraging you to let go. They may challenge your fear of self-assertion, or they may initiate a probe of your relationship with your parents.

Learning to Kick

To kick is to protest. According to Lowen, everyone in our culture has something to protest about. Accordingly, in bioenergetic therapy, you relearn the fine art of kicking.

You do not kick others in the group. In bioenergetic therapy, you learn to express your feelings for the purpose of dealing with your own life, and releasing chronic tensions in your own body. You are not encouraged to take your feelings out on others.

In one kicking exercise, you lie on the mat face down and kick your legs without bending them, or bending them as little as possible. In all exercises, you are beating the mat, never another person. This control, Lowen believes, allows an analytical approach to body work.

Learning to Say "I Hate You!"

Lowen believes in a double-barrel attack on neurosis. He combines body work with verbal work. In one exercise, you are asked to pound the mat saying, "I hate you" or "I'll kill you" or "you bitch" or "son of a bitch!"

Once again, the group participates by encouraging you; they may also comment on any disparity between your facial expression and what you are supposed to be doing.

Learning to Give Support

You will become more assertive if you can give and receive support from the group, Lowen believes. In one exercise, you are asked to lie on the bed with knees bent and head back. You extend both arms and say in an imploring tone of voice, "Please help me!"

Once your request is genuine, the group will respond. You might burst into tears, you might embrace another member of the group. There is a great deal of contact, in a bioenergetic group, between subject and therapist. This takes two forms.

The first is referred to as a "laying on of hands" in recognition of the healing power of physical contact itself. The therapist kneads and softens chronic areas of spasticity in your body.

In the second area of subject/therapist contact, the therapist will hold you or embrace you when you are experiencing any extreme of emotion, or when you request being held.

123

The group is also taught to recognize and knead areas of chronic tension, and to participate in verbal or analytical work. I must stress here that Lowen considers the analytical work a very important part of bioenergetics and essential to correction of neurosis.

Lowen brought body work into the realm of respectability. By de-emphasizing sex and stressing the release of primary emotions, such as anger, pain and fear, he made this work less threatening to large numbers of people. He also pioneered in combining verbal and body work.

Education in Feeling and Purpose

Charles Kelley, another important student of Reich's, took the fusion of body and verbal work a step further. He has noticed a false dichotomy in our culture, between those who value the expression of feeling and those who value purposeful living. He maintains that it is not necessary to choose between the two, that you can have the discharge of profound emotion where it is appropriate and still lead a purposeful life.

In a group at the Radix Institute, where Kelley does his work in feeling and purpose, you have an opportunity to deal with the issues of anger and self-assertion from two vantage points. In the emotional-release groups, you will have an opportunity to express rage, and release body parts that are blocked due to unexpressed feeling.

In the purpose, or self-direction, groups, you

develop your ability to set purposes for yourself and to stick to them. In the emotional-release groups, you develop your ability to become vulnerable. In the purpose groups, you toughen up, learn to stick to your own guns.

The Emotional-Release Group

One of Kelley's students has coined a word, radix, which it is important to understand if you are to understand Kelly's work. Radix, according to Kelley, underlies energy and feeling, and forms a connecting link between the two.

"What is it that pulsates and charges the body, that is blocked from discharge by muscular armor or discharges in orgasm or emotional release?" Kelley asks. It cannot really be called feeling or emotion, though psychologists speak of emotional discharge. At the same time, we cannot really speak of energy, or force; these are words stolen, as it were, from physics. Kelley used the word "radix," meaning root or source, to describe this underlying something. It is this that he wants his group participants to release.

Kelley feels that the muscular armoring described by Reich is a function of man's ability to set purposes. In other words, you are angry with your boss; you also want to keep your job for another two weeks; you therefore armor yourself against your anger in the interests of your longer-range purpose. At the same time, too much of this armoring severely distorts your capacity for feeling.

Your problem: how to reconcile the need to release emotion with your long-range purpose. For a healthy, balanced life, in Kelley's view, you must have both.

The Radix Intensive

Participants describe the intensive as an adventure in feeling. You are not taught what to feel; you release your blocks to feeling what is already there, locked in your body. "The basic choice," says Kelley, "is whether to live fully or not."

You do the intensive in a small group. There is a beginning preparation period, the purpose of which is to establish relations within the group. Verbal and non-verbal encounter techniques are used.

You learn to make eye contact without defending yourself against the intense feelings this arouses. You play at defending yourself in toe-to-toe fights. You learn to accept comfort, connect with others.

Next, the intensive proper begins. Imagine that you are the focus of attention. (Each member in turn becomes the focus for a brief period of time.) The leader may direct the group to massage you in order to move the energy through your blocked areas. You are directed in various breathing techniques, and are instructed to maintain hand and eye contact with members of the group. You are encouraged to surrender to the intense feelings that well up for you; this takes courage. The group's support assists you in letting go.

The leader will give you instructions designed to

bring out spontaneous feelings. He may ask you to produce a certain emotional expression in your face—anger, fear, and so forth. If the leader thinks you are in pain and need to release it, he may ask you to say, "I hurt." He may suggest you call for your mother.

He may direct the group to intensify, by massage, the flow of energy through the body; you may experience this as pleasurable. In any case, the spontaneous discharge of emotion is encouraged.

Learning Self-Direction

Once you increase your capacity to feel, you will have increased your capacity for life as a self-assertive, freely functioning individual. In the self-direction group at the Radix Institute, you put this increased capacity for life to work.

"To realize one's potential, to establish and achieve one's rational objectives, feelings must not only be developed, experienced and expressed, they must be organized and given direction." The energy of even the most expanded consciousness must find its proper creative channel, or else be dissipated and signify nothing, according to Kelley.

"The learning of feeling is a freeing of the self, a progressive unblocking and unfolding of one's creative energy; the learning of purpose is a refocussing and directing of that energy in the service of one's life."

In the intensive, you learn to release your feelings; in the purpose group, you learn what to do, sometimes in spite of your feelings.

"But I already have goals!" you say. Do you? Are they really *your* goals, do they truly relate to the significance of your own life? Or are they goals which have been unconsciously imposed on you by others. In actuality, the pursuit of goals imposed by others is anti-purposive.

Carol's Intensive

Carol, a forty-two-year-old woman, is highly verbal, intellectual, and severely blocked in her ability to feel. She has been unable to reach a spontaneous level of feeling in any previous intensive. Her connection with the rest of the group is weak, as she is the only one in the group who has not been able to achieve this level of feeling.

Some preliminary exercises are done with her—hand passes (massage) and breathing work. She is then put into focus, lying on her back. She is asked by the leader to breathe freely and to look at each member of the group.

"Say, 'I want,' " the leader instructs. "With each breath, give in to any feeling that comes up." Carol does this stiffly at first; then, gradually, the words take on meaning for her.

With each breath, she speaks louder, more expressively, in a higher-pitched voice, with a growing child-like anger. The leader directs, "Keep going, intensify the feeling. Don't force yourself, but if you feel the impulse, go ahead and kick and scream and roll your head from side to side."

Carol's anger builds to a temper tantrum, a spontaneous energy discharge. She screams, kicks, pounds the floor, churns her head from side to side. After her tantrum subsides, Carol is able to make eye contact with the group. Her eyes are bright, she is radiant and lively, her face is ruddy, glowing.

Later on, it is much easier for Carol to express anger directly; she begins to make more solid contact with the group.

Ted's Experience in a Purpose Group

Ted failed to keep a promise to himself about going on a diet. He asks to work on a problem having to do with "not having any will power."

The leader suggests an exercise in which Ted pretends that he is divided, and the critical part of him speaks to the part of him that is refusing to keep the promise. In terms of Gestalt therapy (which Kelley acknowledges has influenced him), this is called a "top dog, underdog" exercise. It goes something like this;

Topdog: "You dumb, sniveling little kid, why can't you do anything right."

Underdog: "You're no fun, quit criticizing me."

Topdog: "Why can't you do a simple thing like stay on a diet."

In this exercise, the subject takes both roles, switching position to facilitate getting into each part. Ted sat up on a chair to be the topdog, and sat on a pillow on the floor to play the underdog role.

129

From this exercise, the group leader was able to get an idea of Ted as a critical, negative person, someone who didn't like himself very much. The leader also knew that Ted was skilled in doing many things which required a high degree of self-discipline. He concluded that something else was the problem.

He had Ted do another exercise, this time using the transactional analysis concept of parent, adult, child aspect of the personality. Any two aspects can have a dialogue, coming to agreement. The parent corresponds to the topdog of the Gestalt view; the child, to the underdog. The adult is the rational/thinking aspect of the personality, the computer which simply processes reality.

The leader discovered that Ted had made a contract with respect to his diet which was not acceptable to his child. He was then instructed to dialogue with his child until they reached an agreement.

To make contracts, to have purpose, it is necessary to contact and involve the whole personality. The feeling level must be fully involved. The leader advised Ted to work on the issue of self-acceptance for the time being, rather than the issue of will power. Ted was instructed to tape record a continuing parent/child dialogue throughout the week.

The Value of Kelley's Work

Kelley combines work in self-direction or purpose with the release of anger. This is the primary value of his work. In primal work, which also stresses release of feeling, the assumption is that when feelings are released, purposeful function will take care of itself. On the other hand, Kelley believes that a person who has not developed purposefulness will need education and direction in that area.

Chapter Eleven

Anger, Self-Assertion, and Personal Growth

On September 21, 1975, I attended a very special workshop. It is special because it combines anger growth work with a total program for personal growth. The anger workshop at the Daniels Institute for Successful Living, in Los Angeles, is the most comprehensive workshop of this kind I have experienced or heard of to date.

The Institute for Successful Living offers a total growth program, including weight-control workshops, business workshops, women's activities, communications weekends, and more. The idea is that any growth program which leaves out a vital area of your life, be it physical, spiritual, financial, intellectual, social or familial, will produce less than the maximum result.

The leaders of the anger workshop are Rannette Daniels and David Sherman. Daniels, a business woman, has been active in the National Organization for Women. In her growth work, she combines techniques from a number of disciplines, including consciousness raising, biocentric therapy, gestalt, bioenergetic therapy, and the Erhard Seminars Training (she was trained by Werner Erhard, the founder, to be a seminar leader).

David Sherman, on the staff of the Institute, also has a private practice in massage and growth work. He had been trained by Charles Kelley, at the Radix Institute, in bioenergetic emotional-release work, and leads the emotional-release portions of the anger workshop.

The Setting and Ground Rules

We are at the Nathaniel Branden offices which the Institute has rented for the day. About twenty people are seated comfortably on pillows and chairs around the room. There is an atmosphere of camaraderie, of sharing, of family. Many of the Institute staff members are in the workshop. Most of the participants know each other, as former experience with growth work and therapy is required for participation.

Rannette Daniels enters and says, "Good morning!" The group answers and you can feel the energy in the room pick up. She goes around the room asking each person what it is he or she is feeling at that moment. Then she begins to talk about the ground rules:

1. You agree to remain in the workshop until the end.

2. There is no entering or leaving the room during processes or sharing.

3. The only breaks are the announced ones.

4. You agree to be back in the room on time after breaks.

5. You agree to participate fully.

6. The ground rules provide an opportunity to choose to be in the workshop and get value from it.

7. You agree to the ground rules.

You discover it is most productive to make the ground rules your own. If you act as if they have been imposed on you and follow them grudgingly, you will get value from the workshop, but not the maximum value.

Getting What You Want

In the next process, Rannette circles the room once again, asking people what they want. People want to be able to express anger more directly, to control seemingly uncontrollable rages, to assert needs more directly and less fearfully.

We are warned against expectations. "You may not feel anger today," Rannette says. "You will get in touch with what is blocking your direct expression of this emotion. For some of you this will be fear; for others, pain; for others, judgments and reasonableness. The workshop is designed to get you in touch with what is in the space of your direct expression of anger. Then you can choose whether or not to move through it."

Fears

We circle the room once again. Rannette asks us all to take turns expressing any fears we have associated with anger. Among the fears are: fear of hostile reaction, fear of frustration, fear that a communication will not be received, fear of violence, fear of seeming wrong; fear of being vulnerable, fear of being manipulated, fear of rejection.

About our fears, Rannette says, "You need to be shitty before you can be clean about your anger. This is something everyone needs to go through. We have been expressing ourselves inappropriately, if at all, for so long, that it is liable to get worse before it clears up."

People express a fear of being crazy. According to Rannette, a person who implies you are crazy when you are angry is using a covert form of intimidation. Usually, that person is also intimidated. We all have a right to be honest about our anger.

Most of our surface fears seem to be rooted in two other fears: the fear of killing or of being killed. The workshop gives us an opportunity to look at the degree to which our lives are run by these two fears—and an opportunity to break the pattern.

Aggression and Assertion

Rannette goes over the definitions of aggression and assertion. "Assertion," she says, "is simply putting out what's so for you." It is a simple statement of identity. You say, "this is the reality of me." "Aggression," Rannette points out, "has force attached to it."

Aggression, not self-assertion, may (or may not) alienate others.

Sentence Completions

We stand up, form another circle, hold hands, close our eyes. We breathe deeply, relax, get in touch with our experience. We are asked to complete this sentence:

"I am a person who . . ."

Some of the responses are: "I am a person who loves, who is frightened, who hates, who is angry, who is anxious, who is silly."

We go on to another sentence completion:

"One of the ways I am indirect about my anger is . . ."

Some of the responses are: ". . . by manipulating, by crying, by forgetting, by acting stupid, by not understanding, by becoming helpless . . ."

Other sentence completions:

"One of the ways I frighten myself about anger is . . ."

"One of the ways I hate my mother is . . ."

"One of the ways I hate my father is . . ."

The purpose of the sentence completion is to begin to open us up to our own experience.

As I have mentioned earlier, saying "no" is crucial to self-assertion. We pair off, are given instructions to choose A and B partners: Simultaneously, one partner says "yes" and the other says "no."

I am paired with Polly, a woman I know well. As she says, "No!" her demeanor changes. She seems more powerful, stronger. Polly is a woman who characteristically looks sad, depressed, neglected, helpless. Suddenly her face is radiant, happy. In the sharing later on, she expresses a fear that she may have hurt me with her anger. I tell her that I was moved, impressed with her growth rather than hurt. She says she was seeing her former husband's face throughout the exercise, that she never expressed anger toward him, that it was a tremendous relief to have it out of her system.

We break for lunch. Rannette suggests that we eat with members of the group. The sharing we do socially is a part of the workshop and increases its value. To the extent that we consider our growth work a "dirty little secret," and walk out of workshops hiding our faces, they will not have value for us.

Insults

After lunch, we do processes concerned with insults. First, we pair up, choose A and B partners again, and begin to insult each other using the foulest language imaginable. It's fun! I feel exhilarated, happy. I love knowing I can take it.

In the next process, we insult each other without using foul language. For me, this presents more of a challenge.

In another process, we pair up and say, "I hate you." With the prior warm-up, I am really able to get into this one. I release a long-repressed rage toward my sister.

We do another process, this one designed to get us in touch with truths we may be avoiding with regard to anger. This process is similar to a directed meditation. We are asked to sit in our chairs, close our eyes, breathe deeply, get in touch with ourselves, and think about the word anger. We do this for about twenty minutes, then take a break and David takes over.

The Horseshoe

David Sherman directs the men and women to separate. Each group forms a horseshoe. A man leaves the other men and walks over to the women. David hands him a batacca.

He kneels in front of a pillow at the open end of the horseshoe and pounds away. The women cheer him on. "Come on, Bob, you can do it, really hit that pillow. Hit! Hit!"

The group supports Bob in releasing his emotion.

When Bob is finished, a woman breaks away from the woman's group, kneels at the open part of the men's horseshoe, and tries to pound. She is having a hard time getting into it. The men appear to be insulting her.

"Come on, you covert idiot," they say, "sneaky anger doesn't work!" In fact, they are supporting her in getting her to be direct.

I found this exercise difficult to do. I was frightened. I asked David for assistance and he told me that the next exercise would help me.

Working on the Mats

We take a brief break. I get to make a few notes, as writing during the horseshoe distracted some of the people.

David and Rannette pair us up, the assistants put mattresses out, and we begin emotional-release work.

We choose A and B partners. I'm with Paul, who has done a lot of emotional-release work. He is the A partner. He works first and I assist him. This is the paired co-confidant technique originated by Kelley.

David directs the exercises. The A partner lies on the mat, breathes deeply. The B partner touches various parts of his body, to assist him in staying in touch with his experience.

"Imagine a person of the opposite sex with whom you have an incomplete communication," David says. "Allow that communication to surface, allow it to come out of your mouth. Allow yourself to express it." Tremendous non-verbal communication is established between the partners. I find that Paul really assists me in completing my own experience, which paradoxically is an incomplete communication with my mother.

This is a very powerful exercise. I hear women screaming, "I'm a woman, not a little girl, see me!" I hear people crying out for love, screaming with rage, sobbing their pain.

We take another break. There is hot chocolate. Somehow this is very comforting, as my own experience in the exercise was extremely painful, and, though I moved through the pain, I am feeling shaky.

Anger and Women

We return to our seats for another chair process. Rannette leads this one. We place our feet on the floor, breathe deeply once again, and begin.

In this process, we make contact with a past experience of anger associated with a woman. Then, little by little, our attention is directed to earlier, similar incidences associated with women. I recall an experience I had totally forgotten, a time when I felt totally betrayed by a librarian who had befriended me. I must have been nine years old. I also feel very sleepy.

Rannette asks us to notice where in our bodies we have stored our anger. I feel even sleepier, and don't really get in touch with anything.

Summing Up

Your experience of anger contains body sensations, thoughts, decisions you have made, concepts, feelings, emotions, memories from the past, considerations, things you have read or heard. The purpose of the workshop is to get you in touch with *your* total experience of anger, from all points of view.

Rannette tells us that we may be very uncomfortable for awhile after the workshop; that it is crucial to press through the discomfort, rather than retreat from it.

She points out that you serve others by getting angry. She asks people in the group to share ways in which they have served others. I recall times when a friend's annoyance has served to get me in touch with reality.

Assertion can also help you get what you want.

We end the workshop at this point. Rannette announces a post-workshop seminar to be held in a week.

The Post-Seminar

At the post-seminar, people share their experiences; they tell what has been happening with them that week. Also, they share feelings about any portion of the workshop they found unsatisfactory.

People report colds, a sense of completion, regret at not having shared fully at the workshop, feeling more assertive, more alive, a renewed ability to cry.

One man, George, reports a shorter time span between feelings of anxiety and knowledge of what triggered it. As a result, he is feeling much more in control of his life.

A woman reports less guilt feelings over anger and self-assertion. Numerous small incidences of expanded ability in the area of self-assertion are reported.

Perhaps the most dramatic report comes from Polly. She has been troubled for years by a sister who uses sickness to dominate her. The sister is a mean woman who has always competed with her, who has hurt her, and who is also a drug abuser.

It fell upon Polly, the week after the workshop, to take this sister to the hospital. The sister begged for barbiturates, in order to escape the experience of going to the hospital. Polly was able to become angry with her sister, to deny her the drugs, and to express some feelings never before communicated.

As for my own experience, I am noticing that when I get angry there is less fear attached to it, and there is less of a residue of unpleasant feelings after expressing it. My experience is much cleaner.

Chapter Twelve

Dissolving Blocks to Self-Assertion

So far, we have seen professionals attack the issues of expression of anger and self-assertion directly. The Reichians literally attack the body, to release the repressed rage and pain. Dr. Bach teaches you how to fight. The assertion-training movement teaches you how to be direct. The Daniels workshops also mount a frontal, if many-sided, attack.

There is another approach. You can learn to dissolve the barriers to assertiveness. Earlier chapters pointed out some of these barriers—the nice guy syndrome, the mind-your-own-business syndrome, the need to control, anger-suppression, and so forth. These barriers have a common denominator; most involve a fear of rejection.

Many therapists deal with rejection as something that somebody else can do to you. They try to teach you how to keep people from rejecting you, and how to reject them back if they do.

Lee Gibson, a Los Angeles counselor and teacher, has a new approach to the problem of rejection. "You are the only person who can reject you," he says. "Another person can only reject the relationship between you. You create the experience of rejection in your life."

Gibson taught for many years in the California public schools. He noticed that intellectual self-confidence, rather than learning per se, was the problem for most school children—and for many adults, as well. He put together a program called learning therapy, and went into private practice.

How Learning Therapy Works

First you are asked which, if any, items in an intellectual self-confidence inventory apply to you:

1. I'm sometimes confused by what I perceive.
2. I'm afraid I don't exhibit a good ability to think quickly and clearly.
3. I'm afraid I can't understand complex materials. I feel like almost everyone else is more intelligent than I am.
4. I'm afraid to use my mind in an intellectual atmosphere.
5. Often, I don't know what I should be feeling in an intellectual setting.
6. I'm afraid I don't express intellectual thoughts.
7. I feel awkward around creative people.
8. I'm afraid not to read. It's my greatest escape.

9. I'm afraid to read. What's the use? I can't retain and recall what I've read.

10. I can't read rapidly, so there are many things I can never know.

What Is Intelligence?

Intelligence is a natural human resource, which increases or decreases with use or disuse. It is your problem-solving mechanism. You have more intellectual potential than you even dreamed about. You don't discover your potential when you lack the ability to assert it.

What Is Intellectual Self-Confidence?

When you can genuinely enjoy the functioning of your mind, you have intellectual self-confidence. You know you can comprehend almost anything, retain it, and use it.

Gibson says: "The major block to developing mental efficiency and intellectual self-confidence is the fear to actively function as an intelligent individual. When a person lacks confidence, he often surrenders to fear. From learning therapy, the person discovers, in himself, a confidence which makes the intellectual fear to function an archaic choice."

What Do You Do in Learning Therapy?

You see Lee Gibson either privately or in a small

group for ten weeks. The experience helps you identify and destroy your blocks to developing intellectual self-confidence.

First you set personal intellectual goals.

These can be in the area of reading, which include:

1. Confidence to comprehend fiction, non-fiction, and technical materials.

2. Ability to retain information.

3. Ability to recall information whenever necessary.

4. Reading speed if desired.

Your personal goals might include test-taking:

1. Confidence to take tests.

2. Methods of test preparation.

3. Techniques for dealing with different kinds of tests.

Other possible goals may involve thinking:

1. Confidence to develop and follow a line of thought.

2. Confidence in forming summaries.

3. Confidence in inductive and deductive reasoning.

4. Confidence in formulating hypotheses.

You develop an understanding of the relationship between your emotions, your past life experiences, and your unwillingness or inability to function intellectually. You must understand your feelings, if you are to have intellectual self-confidence.

But What Do My Emotions Have to Do with My Mind?

When you suppress a powerful emotion, such as anger or pain, your intellectual perceptions are distorted. According to Gibson, "Today, great damage is done when the learning organism is encouraged to fragment itself into emotional and mental components, so the end result is the creation of an emotional 'soul' or a mental 'giant.' To correct this damage, learning therapy incorporates a holistic or Gestalt approach to restore an individual's natural ability to achieve feeling and thinking— i.e., intellectual self-confidence. Learning therapy begins when you become aware of your resistance to learning. With specific exercises, you are assisted in dissolving blocks and replacing them with confidence and skills."

In learning therapy, you become intimately involved with yourself as a learning organism. Learning therapy goes beyond a competence in mechanical skills.

What Is Creativity?

For me, creativity is the ultimate in self-assertion. Earlier, we defined assertion as a simple statement of what's so. Self-assertion is a statement of what's so for you.

Look at some of the definitions of create and creativity in *Webster's New Collegiate Dictionary.* Create: "to invest with new form . . . to produce

147

through imaginative skill." Creation: "the act of bringing the world into ordered existence."

Creative self-assertion involves the ability to assert what is new for you, so others may enjoy it.

Does this mean that the experience of creativity is limited to music, the arts, poetry? No! If you are a plumber, faced with a toilet that doesn't work, and you experience a reordering of the information that you have about plumbing so that you come up with a brand new solution to the problem, you have performed a creative act.

What Stops People from Becoming Creative?

One of the major blocks to creative expression is the notion that creativity is something that some people have and others don't and that what you have to do is get some if you don't have any. In truth, we all have the ability to find creative solutions to problems. Man is not bigger or stronger than the other animals, he has no protection from cold, heat or hunger—except what he can come up with creatively. It is unfortunate that the word "creativity" has come to be used exclusively to refer to the fine arts. This mistake in terminology victimizes many people.

Lee Gibson usually opens his creativity workshop by asking how many people think they need more creativity. Usually, all hands are raised. He replies, "Bullshit! You have all the creativity you'll ever need. What your creativity needs is for you to express it."

Creativity and Self-Confidence

How are creativity and self-confidence in-
tertwined? It is difficult to be spontaneous, to trust
yourself, to allow your creativity its full expression,
if your life is run by the doubting critic at the back
of your mind.

Exercises

One of the first exercises you are asked to do is
list the problems regarding creativity and self-
confidence that you want to resolve. You write
these down in a notebook Lee gives you at the start
of the session.

People wrote: "I want to be able to say what I
think." "I never think what I do is good enough." "I
fear criticism so much that I can't function
creatively."

At the end of the workshop, you use the list to
measure your progress.

You are asked to complete sentences. For instance, "With regard to self-acceptance, I feel . . ."
Some of the responses were: "I feel silly, frightened,
angry, hurt . . ."

Another sentence—"Regarding my self-
confidence . . . " —produced an interesting answer:
"I don't accept how confident I feel."

The final sentence in this exercise was,
"Regarding my creative expression, I feel . . ."
Some of the responses: "I feel silly, angry, I feel I
can't do anything . . . "

149

Creativity and Emotions

You can't assert your creativity if you won't assert your emotions. Lee has designed a number of exercises which allow you to put your emotions down on paper.

In one, which is a great deal of fun as well as being phenomenally valuable, Lee calls out an emotion, and you grab crayons in appropriate colors and begin to draw. This gives you a visual impression of the pattern of your emotions.

Creativity and Criticism

Fear of criticism, and lack of knowledge as to what criticism consists of, are major barriers to creativity. Lee designs exercises for his workshops which help you crash this barrier.

After a directed meditation in which you visualize a picture, Lee has you recreate the picture with pastels. Then you exchange pictures with a partner. Each one of you criticizes the others' picture. You discover that criticism is basically a statement of satisfaction or dissatisfaction on the part of the other person. It is not an eternal judgment on you.

The Fear of Rejection Workshop

Fear of criticism is part of a larger issue, fear of rejection. This is probably the largest barrier to full self-assertion and full self-expression.

Most covert and overt anger games stem from the assumption that if you assert yourself fully, simply, and directly, you will be rejected. So you indulge in games which prevent the other person from rejecting you—rages which don't give anyone an opportunity to say "no" to you; sweetness-and-light games in which you never say "no" to anyone else for fear of being rejected.

What is Rejection?

"Rejection," according to Lee, "is a turning away from or pushing aside." You create an experience of rejection, Lee maintains, when you need to be in another person's space. What you can reject is not another person, but the relationship between you. You experience rejection when you want a relationship with another person that that person doesn't want with you.

Rejection was once an original reaction. That is, at one time in your life, someone, most likely your parents, rejected the relationship you wanted with them. Now, every present relationship you have triggers that original rejection.

The experience of rejection is never a present-centered experience. What happens is that something exists out there in reality—someone wanting a more distant relationship with you than you want with them—and you decide that you're unworthy, bad, inferior, depressed, not pretty, not sexy, not rich enough, and so forth. That decision is your own rejection of yourself. In fact, you can't really reject yourself—it's you there in your own space. You can only make yourself *feel* rejected.

How You Set Yourself Up for Rejection

There are a number of common attitudes, which, if you subscribe to them, become set-ups for rejection:

1. Thinking you need another person.
2. Not being willing to let another person be who he or she is or is not.
3. Thinking that you *must* be important to another person.
4. The feeling of "I'm not good enough."

The Causes of Rejection

1. You know how things ought to be. You make assumptions and never check them out. For example, a man comes home from work and his wife has not cooked dinner. He assumes this means she is angry with him and he creates an experience of rejection. Other possibilities are that the stove is broken, she is ill, or she just didn't feel like cooking dinner.

2. Expectations. You go to a party expecting to meet the man or woman of your dreams. You have a lovely conversation with someone, then discover that he or she has a mate, one very much loved, who happens to be out of town on business. You feel rejected, when, in fact, you did have a good conversation.

3. Prejudice. These are overworked expectations, expectations you are extremely attached to.

4. Interpretation before investigation. This is a big source of rejection. You meet a friend for lunch. She has two creases between her eyebrows. They are not customarily there. You interpret them as an angry frown, and do not ask her whether or not she is angry. You spend the whole afternoon feeling rejected, and wondering whether or not your friend was angry with you. If you had asked her, she might have told you that she was thinking very hard about a magazine article that she'd read earlier.

5. Lack of trust. You imagine that people want to hurt you. You go places and meet people with this expectation. Therefore, you never say what it is that you want, and you never get what you want. You end up feeling unworthy, depressed, feeling rejected.

6. Lack of self-esteem. Here you constantly create the experience of I'm not good enough. What happens is that you feel inferior to begin with, and you reject yourself when things don't go your way out in the world.

7. Needing. When you think you need people, you will inevitably end up feeling rejected by them. Nothing another person does is enough to satisfy your sense of neediness.

The fear of rejection workshop consists of a number of exercises designed to give you a direct experience of the ways in which you create your own rejection.

The "If" Test

This is an especially valuable quiz which Lee designed to get you in touch with the ways in which rejection runs your life.

You answer in writing, the following question: "If I wouldn't feel rejected, I would. . . ."

Some of my answers were: "take care of myself, tell the truth, lie once in a while if necessary, have parties."

On this same quiz, you list the ways in which fear of rejection keeps your life from working. People shared:

"I have people in my life I get little satisfaction from; if I weren't afraid of rejection I would reject them."

"I'm a writer. I get stuck writing my first draft out of a fear of rejection."

"I don't go out and meet new people out of a fear of rejection."

"I don't travel or take vacations for fear that I won't meet anyone to be with."

"I don't dance at parties out of a fear of rejection."

In other exercises in Lee's workshop, you experience being rejected by others and rejecting others yourself. You do a historical analysis of your own experience of rejection so that you really get to see that it is not a present-centered reaction. You get to dramatize rejection and have fun with it in an exercise rejection theater.

In total, you get to short-circuit your rejection machinery so that it never runs you in quite the same way again.

Chapter Thirteen

Coping

You've accepted the book's premise. You've decided to learn to express your anger. Perhaps you've developed your own techniques for self-assertion. Perhaps you are spontaneously letting your anger out. Perhaps you've enrolled in a feminist assertiveness training group, or in Dr. George Bach's fight training. Maybe you've begun a program of Reichian therapy. In any case, you are noticing a change in your everyday life, based on a change in your experience of assertiveness. You may notice that this is not always comfortable. There are pitfalls to any major psychological change.

You've Got to be Dirty Before You Get Clean

Many people won't express anger or assertiveness, even after they have agreed on the value of doing so, because they are afraid they won't be clean about it. They are afraid they will blame instead of assert, have rages, sulk, and so forth.

If you are in Reichian, bioenergetic, or emotional-release work, you may be especially prone to this. If you have never, or seldom, expressed anger before, you need practice. You cannot let the mistakes you make in the initial stages stop you, or all your work will be lost.

You will learn to clean up your messes as you go along, until your expression of anger is clean. For example, Caroline, a lovely woman from Virginia, never expressed her anger. She had learned that nice women just didn't do that. She went into emotional-release work for the purpose of handling depression, and discovered that she expressed it anywhere and everywhere. She had tantrums when her husband wouldn't make love to her, began to take her anger out on her children. Then, at a certain point, she realized that this behavior was unproductive.

She sat down with her husband, and said words to this effect: "I have never in my life expressed anger, desire, or self-assertiveness before this year. I know that the way I'm doing it now is uncomfortable and painful for the rest of the family. However, I think there will be a long-range benefit as I learn to express myself more directly and cleanly." Her husband agreed, as he had found it very difficult to live with her when she was completely passive. Shortly after this conversation, Caroline's rages began to subside.

Sally's newfound anger frightened her best friend, Ann. Ann was used to Sally as a quiet acquiescent type of person. After Sally took a fear of rejection workshop, a whole lot of anger that she had been totally unable to express toward Ann was released. The first time Sally expressed it, it was virtually uncontrollable and the relationship was definitely endangered. This situation frightened Sally so much that she almost regressed back to her earlier, extremely passive state.

What can you do if your anger is new and frightening to the people around you? Even if it is cleanly expressed, others may find it threatening because they are seeing you in a new light. Should you retreat?

Of course not. Keep expressing yourself, and continue to reassure the people around you that your openness will not damage the relationship.

When Your Assertiveness Is Unacceptable to Your Friends

If, up to now, you have not been assertive, some of your relationships may be based on an assumption by others that they will be dominant and you will be submissive.

The case of Bob and Ted is illustrative. Bob is Ted's boss. They have always had an apparently close relationship. Then Ted took an assertiveness-training workshop. He began to stand up to Bob in such areas as refusing to work overtime without adequate compensation, refusing to work weekends. Ted expected Bob to appreciate his new assertiveness, since one of the difficulties in their relationship had been Ted's resentment at unfair conditions. This had been apparent in minor inefficiencies, lateness and procrastination, which were a part of the passive-aggression syndrome Ted went into assertiveness training to resolve.

As Ted became more and more assertive, as he insisted more and more on clear agreements about pay and overtime, Bob became savagely cruel, taking out his anger in strange ways. He would belittle Ted in public, attack his personality, call him selfish and ungrateful. The previous relationship, in which he had been the dominant figure, was necessary for him psychologically. He could not tolerate the change, even if it might ultimately mean a more efficiently run business. Eventually, he fired Ted.

What can you do if your newfound assertiveness puts you in a position similar to Ted's? It is my experience that it is best to let relationships like this fall by the wayside. Your real friends will appreciate your growth, even if it is very uncomfortable for them.

When Your Growth Threatens Others

Your growth might be a reminder to others that they are not growing at the same rate. This was true for Paula and Bill. Paula was in therapy, had done emotional-release work, and assertiveness training. She had done all of this with her husband Bill's enthusiastic support. Up to a point.

Bill started nagging Paula, belittling her work, accusing her of not taking care of their children. When Paula sensed that there was more to Bill's anger than met the eye, she challenged him to sit down with her and discuss things. As it turned out, Bill was beginning to feel dissatisfied with himself as a result of Paula's progress. They decided to budget some money for assertiveness training for Bill.

What can you do if your growth threatens your friends and family? Do not stop sharing your experience of it! Do look at the *way* in which you share your experience. Are you a true believer? Are you somehow implying that your friends are lesser beings because they are not in the same type of therapy you are in?

You can let people know about your growth in a way that shows your appreciation of who they are and the contribution they are making in your life. You can also invite them to participate with you, and have a great deal of fun doing it.